Pillow Talk

Home Decorating and Embroidery Come Together

Pillow Talk

Home Decorating and Embroidery Come Together

Pam Damour
and
Katie Bartz

Publishing
P/S
Solutions

Copyright 2007 by Knapp Press, an
imprint of Publishing Solutions.
Projects Copyright 2005 by Katie Bartz
and Pam Damour.
All rights reserved including the right
of reproduction in whole or in part in
any form.

This book is published by:
Knapp Press/Publishing Solutions LLC
1107 Hazeltine Blvd.
Chaska, MN 55318

President–James L. Knapp
Creative Directors–Katie Bartz,
     Pam Damour
Photography–Katie Bartz,
     Tom Semararo
Illustrations–Katie Bartz
Production–Jim Bindas –
     Books & Projects LLC

Manufactured in Malaysia.

Contents

Words from the Authors

It is always a joy when a dream is fulfilled...it gives you a sense of accomplishment and it makes room for another dream to come true! This book is created in the spirit of sharing the joy and creativity of sewing with others so they can fulfill their dreams.

My Granny Trevis passed away years ago, but I'd like to thank her for her inspiration and planting the seed, which has sprouted and allowed me to spread some seeds of my own in this growing world of sewing! There is a great sense of reward when you pass something dear to you on to others, knowing it will continue through the generations. Thanks Granny!

I would also like to thank my "unique" sewing group: Deb Allemang, Sue Kegley, Cathy Jeske, Judy Masterman, Linda Dahl, Pat Baumer, and Roxane Ramirez-Torres. Without your inspiration and confidence in me, I wouldn't have gotten back into sewing, especially embroidery. I also wouldn't be getting all of those creative ideas that haunt me in the middle of the night! Thanks S&B Girls for that gentle push of love!

About the recipes in this book...food and sewing are synonymous! Pam and I included a few of our favorite recipes so you can enjoy a little treat while you are creating. They are also a reminder to stop sewing and eat, too!

Finally, a special thank-you to my dear friend, Pam Damour. Your knowledge of the home dec industry is unmatched. Even though I'm a pilot, my fear of heights keeps me from climbing the stairs of that high pedestal you put me on. I appreciate your generosity and willingness to tackle this book with me. I thank you in advance for a continued journey....

Katie

For years, I have wanted to write a book that not only provided home dec industry techniques and standards, but also gave inspiration and creativity. I wanted to write a book for the above average sewer looking for new tips and interesting projects, while having fun sewing! I could not have done it without my partner and dear friend, Katie Bartz, who's amazing talents with a computer made this book a possibility. Without you, my dear Kate, this book would still be in my computer, in my head, under my worktable, in my desk drawers, and in the piled-up bins of "ufos" in the workroom.

I would like to dedicate this book to the women of my sewing world: to Grandma Rabideau, who passed away in my arms, but continues to be my sewing inspiration; to my mom, Marie Miller, who gave me my first sewing machine at age six, and always believed in me; to my mother-in-law, Marie Damour, who's forgotten more about sewing than I'll ever know; to my daughter Leah, who shares my passion for creating; to Sue Hausmann, who gave me a chance, when no one wanted home dec classes; and finally, to Nancy, Monica, and Jenny, my coworkers, who picked up the slack while Katie and I were working long hours on this book.

And finally, a simple thank-you to my husband and best friend, Joe, who is always in support of my projects.

Pam

Foreword

What better joy than to create for your home. To actually make your own special pillows and ottoman and then—"sew" much more—having fun using the fabrics and trims you have chosen!

Authors Pam Damour and Katie Bartz have merged their talents in this exciting new book, PILLOW TALK. Pam has operated a professional home decorating business for years, and more recently, has traveled all over the world teaching home sewers to create beautiful home decorations using her professional techniques. Katie is an avid sewer who has owned a business involved in the computer and technology industry. When she began creating projects using embroidery software on her own home sewing and embroidery machine, she combined her computer and sewing expertise and was hooked. She has since begun traveling to educate and train home sewers and embroidery enthusiasts on various embroidery software programs. Together, Pam and Katie are a powerful team, combining their years of experience to show you how to create for your home—beautifully and professionally.

As you create some or all of the projects in this book, you will find clear instructions, step-by-step photos of the techniques, and patterns

and designs tested not only by Pam and Katie, but also by their students. There is a project for everyone—personalized gifts or colorful pillows for kids' rooms you can make with your children or grandchildren. Many of the projects are personalized with monograms, embroideries, trims, piping, and other techniques that you will learn to do quickly and easily.

Have you been dreaming of redoing your home? Start with one room. Once you have chosen a few pillows from this book, take the book with you to your favorite home decorator fabric store and choose the fabrics and supplies that reflect your personality and dreams. Then, after just a few afternoons or evenings, your home will glow with the special accessories you have created to make your dreams come true! There is no limit to what you can do with your sewing machine and your creativity.

Read on and be ready to be inspired!

Sue Hausmann
Host of "America Sews" and "America Quilts Creatively"

About Pillows

Adding pillows or cushions, as they are called in some countries, is one of the most fun, creative, and least expensive ways of changing your home décor. Pillows can create a mood, tell a story, or make you laugh. They can make you feel warm and pampered—people can get very attached to their pillows!

Pillows can be any size or shape—the possibilities are endless. And they can be filled with polyester fiber, feathers, down, a blend of feathers and down, or kapok, which is a natural fiber. Polyester fiber is the best for people with allergies, and kapok can be a nice alternative to down and is less expensive.

When making pillows, ask yourself these simple questions:

- Is this a pillow that will have daily use?
- How long do I want this pillow to last?

Choose your fabric carefully.

- Is the fabric washable?
- Is the fabric UV protected?

Generally, if you're using a good-quality fabric treated with a commercial sunscreen, by the time your pillow needs cleaning, it's worn enough to need replacing. However, if the fabric is a fine embroidered silk, with or without lace, perhaps the pillow should be in a room where there's limited use.

But whatever fabric, trim, or fill you decide upon, make the pillows in this book as a little luxury you give to yourself and your loved ones!

Here are some simple guidelines for using this book:

All of the instructions are written for 54"-wide home decorating fabrics. If you are using fabrics other than the normal 54" width, you will have to adjust your patterns accordingly. Home decorating fabrics work best, as they are treated to be fade resistant, water repellent, and soil resistant. Although you can use any fabrics you choose, home decorating fabrics will generally outlast other fabrics. If you're using a thin or lightweight fabric, you may want to line this fabric with drapery lining or muslin before making your pillow. Many of these pillow designs can be made from scrap fabrics and/or remnants, so they shouldn't be expensive to make.

Choose quality thread. We use Mettler sewing thread, a fine-quality, long-staple polyester thread. All of our embroidery thread, bobbin thread, and stabilizers are available from Sulky® of America.

Choose quality pillow forms that completely fill your pillow covers.

The zippers used in these projects are an upholstery-weight available by the yard. If you need a source for finding this zipper tape, please visit www.pamdamour.com, or www.kjbartz.com for more information.

Remember, pillows...
Are not fattening!
Are not invasive!
Don't expect anything from you!
Provide unconditional cuddling!
Don't tattle!
Make you feel pampered!
Are great listeners as well as conversation starters!
And...are just plain "good stuff"—no pun intended!

We hope that you enjoy this book, with its great projects, funny stories, recipes, and CD-ROM in the back, which contains all the patterns and embroidery designs used in the book. Katie and I have worked very hard on this book so use the gorgeous monograms everywhere, and try the other embroideries in your other areas of sewing. We had so much fun writing this book, completing each others' sentences, and simultaneously breaking out in song, that we're sure you'll enjoy reading it and making the projects, too. So create a little affordable elegance! You deserve it!

Katie's Embroidery Tips

The best overall tip I can give in regards to machine embroidery is to relax and have fun! Machine embroidery is very addictive. Once you start, look for the nearest "Embroiderer's Anonymous Support Group"—I'm sure I'll run into you there!

Seriously, embroidery is that extra-special something that makes a project so personal. And having the right notions to do your embroidery will make it that much more professional and problem-free! There are so many techniques for "doing proper embroidery" that when all is said and done, following a few simple rules will make you a pro in no time.

Let's begin with the stabilizer. The stabilizer is the foundation, the backbone in embroidery. Not having the proper stabilizer can make a wonderful project go sour quickly. You wouldn't build a house on twigs when you could use a brick foundation would you?

Stabilizers have two purposes in the world of embroidery. First, stabilizers keep the fabric from stretching, as all fabric stretches to some degree, and secondly, they hold the stitches, as the stabilizer is usually denser than the fabric itself. It allows the embroidery to hold more stitches in the fabric, as well as denser designs.

Let's see if I can give you a few basic concepts to follow.

● If your fabric is stretchy, such as a knit, rayon, or loose weave—one that will distort easily when sewn—you want something to keep your fabric from stretching while it's being embroidered. Thus the purpose of a stabilizer! A cut-away or iron-on, tear-away stabilizer is a great choice in this instance. Either stabilizer will keep the fabric from puckering and allow for stable stitching on denser designs. These stabilizers have fibers running in all directions to keep your fabric stable, no matter what direction the design is being embroidered.

In this book, when we refer to a cut-away or iron-on stabilizer, we have used the following products on our less-stable home decorating fabrics: Sulky® Cut-Away Plus™ stabilizer or Sulky® Totally Stable™ Iron-on Tear-Away Stabilizer. You will want to gently tear-away or cut-away the stabilizer after the embroidery is completed, per the manufacturer's instructions.

• If your fabric is less stretchy and is a more tightly woven fabric such as moiré, cotton, or denim, using one or two layers of tear-away stabilizer will do the trick. Since the fabric is more stable by itself, you just need a foundation stabilizer to help you maintain a distortion-free design. Tear-away stabilizers work well for satin stitching, edge work, and monograms, and can handle dense embroidery designs as well.

We have used Sulky® Tear-Easy™ Soft, Lightweight, Tear-Away on the back of the fabric on our more stable home decorating fabrics in our projects. We used Sulky® Paper Solvy, which dissolves in water, on the back of the IT'S PARTY TIME project to create the fringe along the border. We didn't want any stabilizer remaining when the project was completed.

On to Hooping:

To hoop or not to hoop, that is the question! Everyone develops their own personal preferences for hooping fabric for their embroidery.

Hooping your fabric or hooping just the stabilizer is your choice. What's important is that you center the fabric correctly in either case. If you hoop your fabric, make sure not to stretch or distort the fabric as the embroidery will "lock" the distortion in place when you take the embroidery out of the hoop. You want your fabric to be taut but not stretched in the hoop. This just takes practice, so hang in there!

The stabilizer behind the fabric is what you want to be snug—remember, the stabilizer is the foundation of your work. We don't want any puckering here. If you have a fabric that might be sensitive to the marks left by the hoops, hoop your stabilizer first and machine-baste/fix or spray-baste your fabric to the stabilizer. If I'm using Sulky® KK2000 adhesive spray, I like to spray a very light coating on the back of my fabric and then put the fabric on the hooped stabilizer. Usually a quick spray on the back of the fabric's design center is enough to adhere to the stabilizer and get me started. I then simply align my embroidery alignment mark to the hoop's alignment mark...it's magic!

The Eye of the Needle:

Needles are critical to the success of any embroidery. Using a needle specific to embroidery does make a difference in the resulting project. If you're using metallic thread in any of these projects, I encourage you to use a metallic needle to discourage thread breakage and fraying. The actual construction of the home decorating projects in this book can be sewn with a denim needle, size 90 or 100. And, oh yes, don't forget to change your needle OFTEN!

Basic Techniques

The Cut

Making the first cut into the fabric is always the hardest for most of us, but rest assured, to my knowledge, fabric has never bitten anyone…so, go for it!

In our workroom, we always use a pillow template when cutting our pillows. This provides us with accurate sizes, as well as the ability to center the pattern or motif of the pillow, and get a visual of how the finished project is going to look.

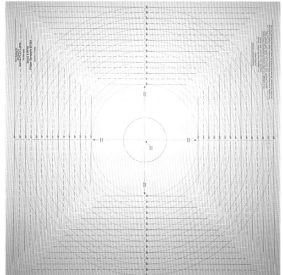

To do this, position the template on the fabric, making sure to allow for any seam allowances. Just a note: In home decorating, we always use a ½" seam allowance. Why? It's just easy math!

Mark your cutting lines by drawing in the cut-out corner slots. Draw straight lines from corner mark to corner mark. This is your cutting line. Use a chalk liner when drawing your lines, so in the case of an error, the lines can be removed easily.

Cut the front and back of the pillow to match. Your pillow should look as pretty on the back as it does on the front.

After cutting out both front and back, cut a zipper placket 2" wide by the cut width of the pillow. The zipper will be inserted in the back, along the bottom edge. Although the placket is an optional feature, it's easier to insert a zipper along an edge which may have cording and/or a ruffle or flange than it is to insert the zipper inside the bottom edge seam. However, both methods are acceptable.

Press ½" seam allowances on both the placket and the bottom edge of the pillow back.

The zipper will be sewn in, using the Placket Insertion instructions found on page 28.

Dog ears are cute on Pam's dog, Chrissie, but not on pillows—unless it's our tassel pillow project (TASSELS ABOUND) with intentional "extreme dog-ears".

To prevent dog-ears, we advise that you taper the corners of the pillow. It's not necessary to trim the bottom edge of the pillow, as this is the side that will not be visible when the pillow is sitting on a bed or sofa.

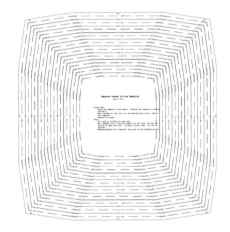

You can taper the dog-ears yourself, or use a tapered pillow template as a guide, when initially cutting out your pillow. Unlike the 24" pillow template on the previous page, the tapered template will factor in the seam allowances, as well as the dog-ears. Note: These templates are available on the notions order form found on the book CD-ROM.

Here is an illustration of a tapered pillow template.

The Feet

Having the appropriate sewing foot when you're working on a project can surely make all the difference in the world. Imagine trying to hammer in a nail with a high-heeled shoe...granted, it can be done, as I'm sure some of you have tried it, but using a hammer sure makes a difference! Using the right tool, like using the right foot, gives you more consistent, professional results.

The Ruffler

The rufflers shown here do exactly the same thing, even though they look slightly different, per manufacturer. The ruffler is an essential tool if you're creating pleats or ruffles in your projects. It's a must in general and home dec sewing!

Husqvarna Viking
Designer 1

Husqvarna Viking
1+

Bernina

The Edge Joining Feet

These feet with the center rudder were designed to join two pieces of fabric together, or to join trim to a fabric at the edge. However, we use it to stitch along an edge for alignment. This can be done by adjusting your needle position or stitch width.

Husqvarna Viking

Pfaff

Bernina

The Edge Stitching Feet

These feet with the side rudder are an excellent tool for guiding along the edge of fabric or trim to keep the stitching even. It's also the foot we use to make the tubing for the FLOWER POWER project.

Husqvarna Viking

Pfaff

Bernina

Zipper Feet

Zipper feet can vary quite a bit in looks, but their purpose is the same, which is to allow the needle to sew along the side of the foot close to the edge of zippers and trims. There are, however, as many types of zipper feet as there are different types of zippers. Zipper feet can also be used to make welting, if a welting foot is not available.

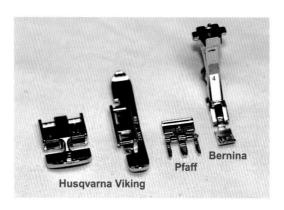

Husqvarna Viking

Pfaff

Bernina

Husqvarna Viking   Pfaff   Bernina

Single Welt Foot

This foot, which sports a deep groove on the bottom left side, is designed to hug welt cord as fabric is wrapped around it, creating welting. The fabric is cut on the bias, and the seam allowances are referred to as the "lip". If your sewing machine company doesn't make a welting foot, a zipper foot can be used, although sometimes the quality is not the same.

Husqvarna Viking   Pfaff

Double Welt Foot

Similar to the single welt foot, the double welt foot has two deep grooves on the bottom, so that double welting can be made and applied easily to a project.

Making Continuous Bias

Continuous bias is a term that refers to the technique where fabric is sewn into a tube, then cut in a spiral fashion to create bias strips in a very fast efficient manner. It requires no more fabric than cutting straight-of-grain strips of fabric.

Begin with a square or rectangle of fabric. We're showing a rectangle, as most of the time your fabric will be rectangular. Remember that a square is just a rectangle with four equal sides. Trim off a 45° angle of fabric as shown.

Slide the triangle over to the other side.

With right sides together, sew the pieces together using a ½" seam allowance.

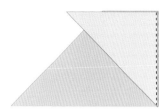

Press the seam open creating a parallelogram.

Draw lines, on the *wrong* side of the fabric, the width of your desired bias strips. Number your strips as shown.

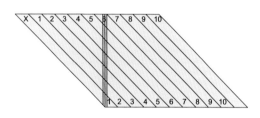

Cut about 2" on the line between the "X" and #1.

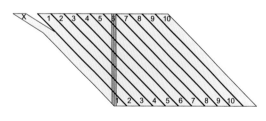

With right sides together, pin making sure like-numbered strips are aligned and stitch a ½" seam. Press all seams open and flat. Cut on the drawn lines to create an easy, uniform continuous bias strip.

This bias technique can be used to cut strips for single welt cord, double welt cord, ruffles, ruching, shirred welting, bias binding, and banding.

Use these math formulas for calculating
the yardage necessary for continuous bias:

_____ x _____ ÷ _____ = _____ ÷ 36 = _____

length of bias   width of bias   width of material   amount in inches   amount in yards

OR: if you have a piece of fabric and want
to know how much bias it will yield:

_____ x _____ ÷ _____ = _____ ÷ 36 = _____

length of fabic   width of fabic   width of bias needed   total bias in inches   total bias in yards

Making Welting

Let's face it, home decorating sewers use their own little language. In the garment world of sewing, it's called piping; in the home decorating world, it's called welting. Cording refers to a twisted cord with or without a lip, but if it's covered in fabric, it's welting.

To make welting, it's critical that you cut your fabric on the bias. Using the continuous bias method just discussed can speed-up the process in creating the bias strips. Refer to the Making Continuous Bias instructions beginning on page 18 to make continuous bias. The width of the bias strip will be determined by the thickness of the welt cord. The most common ¼" welting requires a 2"-wide bias strip, where as a fatter welt cord requires wider bias strips. You will want to measure around your cord and add an extra 1" for seam allowances.

Once you've made the appropriate bias strips, fold the fabric in half over the welt cord. Using either a single welt foot or zipper foot will give you the professional results you're looking for. Sew the fabric

Hint: Don't pull the bias strip or hold it taut when making welting as this will make the welting loose and sloppy. Hold your bias flat, allowing the sewing machine to feed it naturally. If the bias strip begins to ripple or torque, pull the bottom edge of the fabric slightly until the fabric lies flat again.

snugly close to the welt cord.
After the welting is made it's ready to insert.

Turning Corners with Welting

When turning a corner with welting, you must first clip the welt's seam allowance at the pillow's corner. It's important to clip all the way to the stitching line, as clipping too little will prevent a sharp corner.

Hint: Clip where the welt is to turn the corner, and then clip ¼" above and below the corner.

Pivot ½" from the corner and use a stiletto to gently push and tuck the welt cord to the left of the needle. Easing in a little extra welting will give you a nice square corner.

Splicing the Welting

Whenever there is a start and stop point of the welting, it must be joined. This join is called a "splice" in the home decorating world. To create a seamless splice, first trim the starting end at a 45° angle and trim the overlapping welting straight across, leaving approximately a 2" overlap.

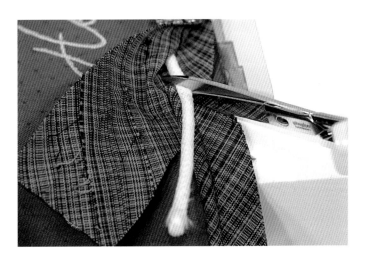

Remove the stitches on the straight-cut end of welting about 2½". Butt the cords together and trim the straight-cut cord at a 45° angle to match the other cord.

Fold the end of the fabric under and wrap it around the welting to cover the spoiled ends.

Finish sewing the spliced welting in place. Trim off any fabric ends in excess of the ½" lip on the welting.

Following this splicing technique will give you the professional results you're looking for!

Making Double Welting

When making double welting, there are a few key things to remember.

● Double welting is topstitched to a project, in contrast to single welting which is inserted into a seam.

● When using ¼" welt cord, cut your bias strips 2 ½" wide, rather than 2" used for single welting.

● You need twice as much welt cord (we did say double welting, didn't we?)

● You need a double welt foot, which has two deep grooves on the bottom to hold each side of the double welting while sewing.

● Invisible polyester thread works best in the bobbin when making double welting.

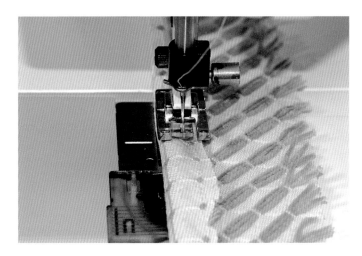

Using your double welt foot, begin sewing as you would with single welting, on the left side, but only wrap about ⅓ of the bias strip over the cord. Stitch down the first side of the welt cord.

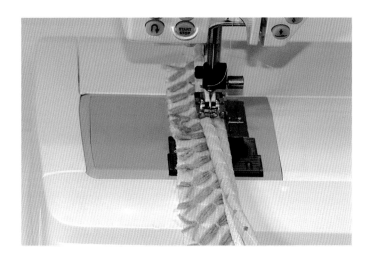

Turn and, working from the opposite end of the sewn welting, insert the second welt cord to the right side, wrapping the remaining bias strip over the second welt cord, as shown. The double welt foot will hold each welt cord in its appropriate track thus keeping everything nice and snug while you sew it together.

Trim off the remaining bias strip close to the stitching line. This will be on the wrong side of the double welting.

Turn the welt right side up with the raw edge side down and admire your work! You will topstitch the double welt to your project with the raw edge hidden.

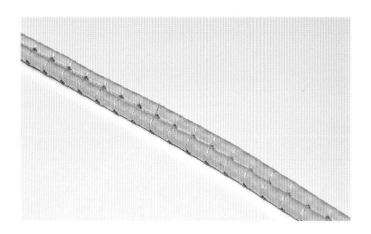

Shirred Welting

Shirred welting looks the best when made with a ruffler. Cut your bias strips ½" wider than normal, for the size welt cord you are using. The length of the bias strip should be three to four times the finished length of shirred welting. Use the continuous bias formula on page 20 for calculating how much yardage and bias you'll need.

Using your ruffler, with the lever on 1 and with the set screw tightened three-quarters of the way, ruffle each side of the bias strip, as shown, leaving a ⅜" seam allowance.

After both sides are ruffled, wrap the strip around the welt cord and sew with a zipper foot close to the welting to complete the trim. This trim can now be inserted into your favorite project.

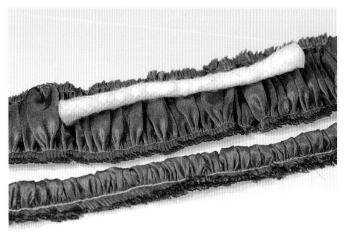

Inserting Twisted Cord

To sew purchased twisted cord there are few tips to remember.

● Remember to sew the cord to the right sides of your fabric.

● Leave the ends of the twisted cord taped so they won't come apart.

● When splicing, separate the twisted cord from the lip by removing the stitches.

● When splicing, you may need to sew in the opposite direction, to keep the splice smooth.

Starting in the center along the bottom edge of the pillow, begin

sewing the twisted cord to the pillow top leaving approximately 2" of twisted cord free at the beginning.

Clip into the lip at the corner, as instructed before in Turning Corners with Welting, before sewing the twisted cord to the corner.

To splice the trim at the end, sew until the two ends butt up to each other and create a "wall".

Remove the stitching from the lip of the cord.

Overlap the cord in the direction of the twist.

Sew the cord overlap in place. *Note*: You may have to change your direction of sewing, as well as mirror-image your needle position, so that you are sewing in the direction of the twist.

The result is a virtually hidden splice with your twisted cord.

BASIC TECHNIQUES

Zipper Insertion
Which style of zipper insertion to choose?

In this book, we describe three types of zipper insertions so that you may choose the style best for you and your project.

Placket Insertion

To give your pillow a professional flair, it's a preferred practice to place a placket at the bottom edge of the pillow, though it's a personal choice. Why not just put the zipper along the bottom edge? It's more difficult to sew in a zipper along an edge when there's also welt cord, ruffles, ruching, and other trims. By placing the zipper along the edge in a shallow placket, that extra 1/4" or so gives you enough room to complete the project professionally.

After cutting your pillow front and back the same size, cut an additional 2"-wide strip of fabric the width of the pillow back, using the same grain line as the bottom edge of the pillow. This 2" piece will be used for the zipper placket.

Press under a 1/2" seam allowance on the top edge of the placket and the bottom edge of the pillow back. You can serge the edges prior to pressing under if you'd like a cleaner finish inside.

Cut the zipper tape to the needed length and sew the folded placket edge close to the zipper teeth. The zipper foot should be attached on the left side, hanging off the right side, with the needle position all the way to the left.

After stitching the zipper to the placket, reattach the zipper foot to the other side, and move the needle to the far right position. Place the pillow back fabric over the zipper to create a flap, keeping the zipper foot next to the zipper; topstitch the back in place.

Separate the zipper several inches and insert the slide. Leave the slide near the center of the pillow.

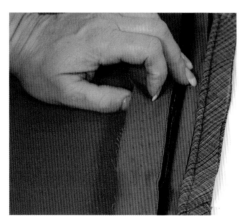

With right sides together, lay the pillow front on top of the pillow back. Trim the back to match the size of the pillow front, leaving about ½" to ¾" of placket remaining to be sewn into the seam. The goal is to make the zipper appear as if it is along the bottom edge of the pillow.

Sew the pillow back and front together, using a single welt foot for easier sewing and a more consistent seam allowance. Trim the corners and clean-finish the seams. Open the zipper and turn the pillow right side out.

Rise Insertion

When making a box-style cushion, the height of the cushion is referred to as the "rise". Sewing a cushion with a rise requires a different zipper insertion, as the cushion cover requires a larger opening for the cushion insert. Generally, the zipper on a box-style cushion requires some extra length to travel a few inches around a corner as well as the entire back edge. Be sure to allow about 8" of extra fabric all the way around for ease in the rise.

Cut the rise 1" deeper than the thickness of the cushion foam. For the zipper placket, cut two rises each the depth of the front rise. For a standard rectangular cushion, the zipper portion of the rise should be the entire back of the cushion, plus travel around two corners. Allow 4" to 6" for each end of the zipper in addition to the back width of the cushion.

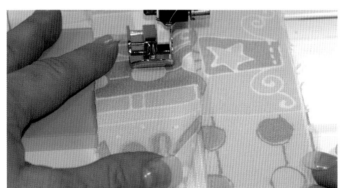

Fold the rise in half lengthwise, with wrong sides together. Sew with the folded edge close to the zipper teeth. The zipper foot should be attached on the left side with the needle position all the way to the left.

After stitching the zipper down, reattach the zipper foot to the other side of the ankle and bring the needle to the far right position. Overlap the fabric slightly to create a flap and topstitch in place.

Separate the zipper a couple inches and insert the slide. Place the slide in the center of the zipper to continue.

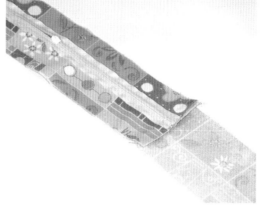

After your slide has been inserted, sew the "closed" end of the zipper, with right sides together and raw edges even to the other section of the rise.

Starting at the center front of the cushion, matching any pattern in the fabric, sew the rise to the cushion top all the way to the corner. Snip the rise ½" at the corner and turn the corner. Continue sewing halfway down the side. Sew the other side of the front in the same manner.

Hint: Making one ½" snip where the corner will be will ensure a nice square finish.

To sew the back of the cushion, start at the center back and sew to the corner, matching patterns if possible. The rise front and back will meet at the sides. Snip the seam allowances at the corners of the rise to ease turning.

At the sides, where the front and back rises meet, leave an excess of a few inches and fold over to create ease. This will make it much easier when sewing to the other side of the cushion. Fold the flap over as shown here. The excess ease you've allowed will also create a "pocket" for the zipper slide to hide and give you a very professional finish.

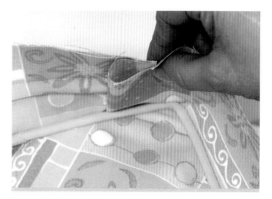

BASIC TECHNIQUES

After the rise has been applied to one side of the cushion, notch the opposite side of each corner of the rise to make your alignment markings for the other side. Pin the other side of the cushion in place, using your notches as guides to match the cushion corners. Sew the other cushion piece to the rise. You may find that the cushion edge may be too large or too small. Do not let your corner alignments move, as this will create a cushion with twisted corners. Stretch, ease, and pin, until it all fits properly.

Sew all the way around the cushion and serge the seam allowances to finish. Open the zipper and turn the cushion right side out. Insert the cushion form.

Bottom Edge Insertion

The Bottom Edge insertion is used when there's no trim to get in the way of a zipper, or when there are two or more trims, and it's easier to hide a zipper in the bottom seam between trims. It's a cleaner application, but with trims involved, it can be a bit trickier. It's also the

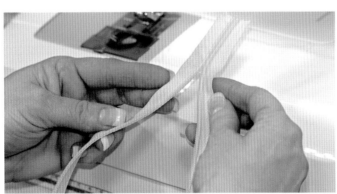

best technique to use for a totally concealed zipper, as invisible zippers aren't used in the decorating industry.

When making a bottom edge insertion, cut the desired length of zipper tape. Separate the zipper tape, so that each side can be sewn individually as shown.

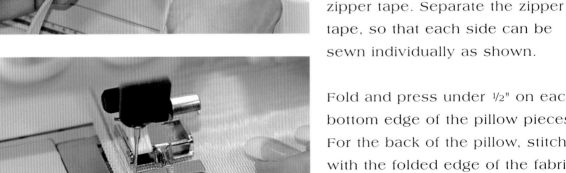

Fold and press under ½" on each bottom edge of the pillow pieces. For the back of the pillow, stitch with the folded edge of the fabric close to the zipper teeth and the zipper foot and the needle position on the left, as shown.

For the front piece, attach the zipper foot to the right side of the ankle and adjust the needle position to the right to keep the stitching close to the zipper. Sew, with the teeth side down, leaving about ¼" of the fold extending beyond the edge of the teeth. This will create a flap covering the teeth once the zipper has been joined back together.

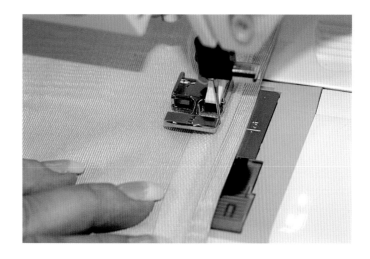

Using the zipper slide, merge the zipper teeth back together by zipping the slide through twice. The first zip will merge the zipper back together, and on the second zip, position the slide in the center, with both zipper ends sealed.

With right sides together, sew the remaining three sides of the pillow together. Trim the corners and serge the seam allowances. Turn the pillow right side out by opening the zipper.

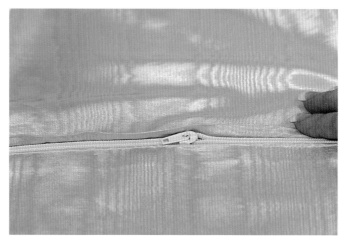

Young
At
Heart

Crunchy Chocolates

Katie says she didn't inherit the cooking gene like her sisters, Holly and Marne. But when she isn't off on an adventure or sewing, she likes to fiddle in the kitchen. Here's an inspired recipe she likes to whip up during the holidays or keep on hand when her sewing buddies stop by!

1 cup packed brown sugar
1 cup light corn syrup
1 cup peanut butter (no reduced fat here)
2 cups cornflakes
2 cups crispy rice cereal
$1/2$ cup finely chopped peanuts
$3^{3}/4$ cups semisweet chocolate chips
$1^{1}/2$ teaspoons shortening
Candy sprinkles

In a heavy saucepan, combine brown sugar, corn syrup and peanut butter. Cook and stir over medium heat until mixture is smooth. Remove from heat; stir in cereals and peanuts.

When cool enough to handle, drop by spoonfuls onto waxed paper-lined baking sheets. Form into shapes of your choice: circles, eggs, hearts, squares. Refrigerate until firm. In microwave or double-boiler, melt chocolate chips and shortening, stirring until smooth. Dip shapes into chocolate allowing excess to drip off. Place back onto waxed paper. Decorate with sprinkles and let stand until set. Makes about four dozen creative, crunchy chocolates!

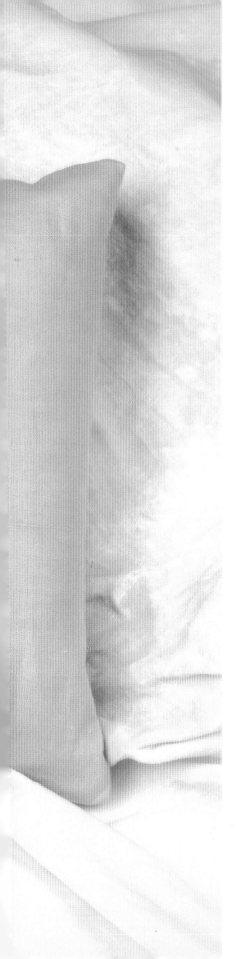

Flower
Power

This cute flap pillow combines a corded edge with fun embroidery to remind us of days gone by. Being products of the '60's, Katie and I love the retro look of this pillow. Katie has even included a smaller flower for embroidering your covered button!

Materials:

- ½ yard of solid green linen
- ⅓ yard of white linen
- ¼ yard of coordinating print
- Dritz® half ball covered button kit, size 60
- 12" x 16" pillow form
- ¾ yard of ¼" welt cord
- Single welt foot
- Edge stitching foot
- Fasturn® tool
- Hemostats

Embroidery Supplies:

- Hoop Size: 240mm x 150mm for large design; 100mm x 100mm for button cover
- Stabilizer: One to two layers of Sulky® Tear-Easy™ Soft, Lightweight, Tear-Away
- Three colors of coordinating rayon embroidery thread

Cut:

From the green linen, cut one 13"x31" rectangle. From the white linen, cut two 9"x14" pieces plus one 3" square for the covered button.

1. Select the Flower Power design found on the CD-ROM compatible to your sewing and embroidery machine. Center the design on one of the white 9"x14" rectangles. After completing the embroidery, trim both pieces of white linen fabric to 8"x13"; press.

2. Make 13" of welt cord from the coordinating print fabric following the Making Welting instructions beginning on page 20 of this book. With right sides together, sew the welt cord along one long edge of the embroidered white linen, matching the raw edges.

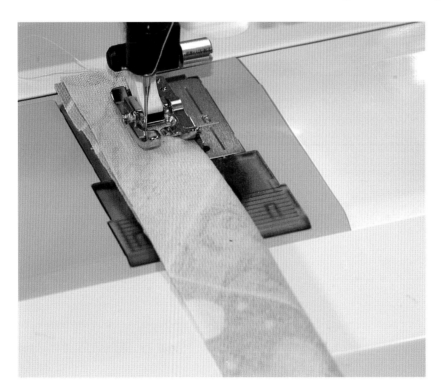

3. With 6" of bias and cord, make a covered button loop using the Fasturn® tool. This is done by sewing $3/8$" from the folded edge of the bias. To make sewing this easier, we use a presser foot with a flange on the right side (edge stitching foot). Move your needle to the left and stitch with the fold pressing against the flange.

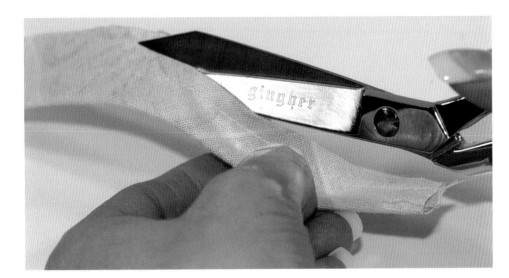

4. Trim the seam allowance to ¼" before turning.

5. Using a Fasturn® tool, follow the manufacturer's instructions to turn the tube right side out as you insert a welt cord.

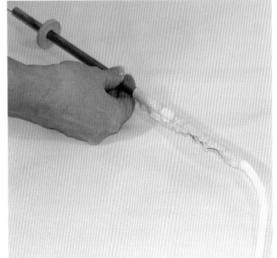

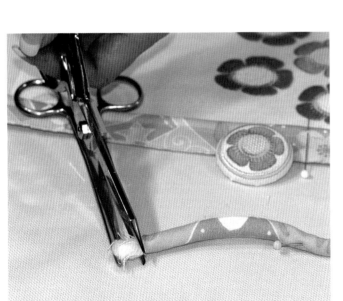

6. Using the hemostats, pull ½" of welt cord out of each end and trim the cord only. This will keep seam allowances flat on the ends of the corded welting when sewing to the pillow.

7. Adjust the length of the loop to fit your button. We made ours so that the loop would surround the outer edge of the button.

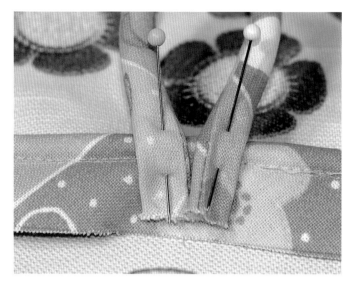

8. With right sides together, sew the other 8"x13" white linen fabric, used as lining, to the embroidered section. Stitch along the corded edge as shown. Using your welt foot can help with this step.

9. With wrong sides together, press the flap flat.

Optional: If you wish to embroider your button, as we did, embroider the fabric first using the embroidery design found on the CD-ROM. Then follow the manufacturer's instructions to complete the button.

10. Place the embroidered piece and the green linen right sides together. Serge the edges together with a 3- or 4-thread serger stitch.

11. Clean-finish the other end of the green fabric with the serger. Fold the fabric in thirds like an envelope, with the embroidered section inside. Sew the sides and serge to clean-finish the seams.

12. Trim the corners and turn the pillow cover right side out; press. Stuff with a 12"x16" pillow form. Be proud of your work well done!

Petal Pusher

This is a fun little pillow which can double as a pajama bag for your favorite girl! It's a simple, basic, round pillow with flower petals added. We've also added a layer of batting inside each petal to give them extra body, but you can leave them flat if you wish.

Materials:

- ½ yard of print fabric for body
- ¼ yard of coordinating print for petals
- ¼ yard of felt or thin, quilt batting
- 1 yard of twill tape or grosgrain ribbon
- 10" zipper tape with slide
- 12" round pillow form (or stuffing to fill pillow)
- Zipper foot
- Edge stitching foot
- Fabric marking pen or chalk

Cut:

Copy the pattern pieces on your computer's printer from the CD-ROM. Cut out all the pillow pieces following the layout shown here and transfer all markings. Cut six petal pieces from the felt or thin batting.

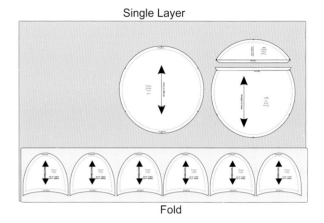

Single Layer

Fold

1. With right sides together, layer two petal pieces with one piece of felt or batting on the bottom. Sew each petal using a $1/2$" seam allowance, leaving the bottom edge open for turning.

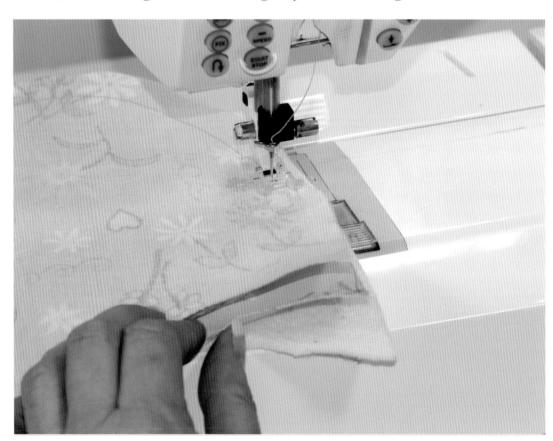

2. After stitching all the petals, trim the seam allowances to a ¼". This will allow you to turn the petals inside out and have a smooth edge.

3. Turn each petal right side out and press flat. Topstitch around the sewn edges. Baste the open bottom edges together and clip along this edge as shown.

4. With right sides together and raw edges even, pin the petals around the pillow front circle. They should fit fairly close (which was just a fluke when we were making the patterns. I guess even a blind squirrel can find a nut once in a while!) If you need help with placement, use the notches on the pattern front to line up each petal.

5. Press under the bottom edge of the pillow back top ¹/₂" and press. Also, press under ¹/₂" on the top edge of the pillow back bottom (zipper placket). Insert the zipper, following the Placket Insertion instructions found on page 28.

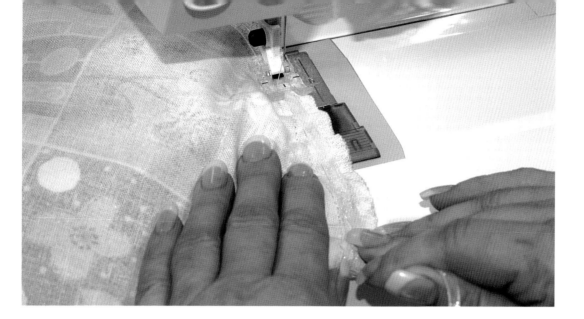

6. Sew the pillow front to the back, lining up the notches. Sew all the way around. The trick to keeping the edge of a round pillow smooth and straight is to slightly gather the edge as you sew. Before turning right sides out, sew twill tape or grosgrain ribbon over the seam allowances pulling taut as you sew. This will slightly gather the outside edge, giving the pillow a better shape.

Clean-finish the seam allowances with your serger to prevent fraying. You'll be able to turn the pillow and watch it "bloom" when opening up the zipper.

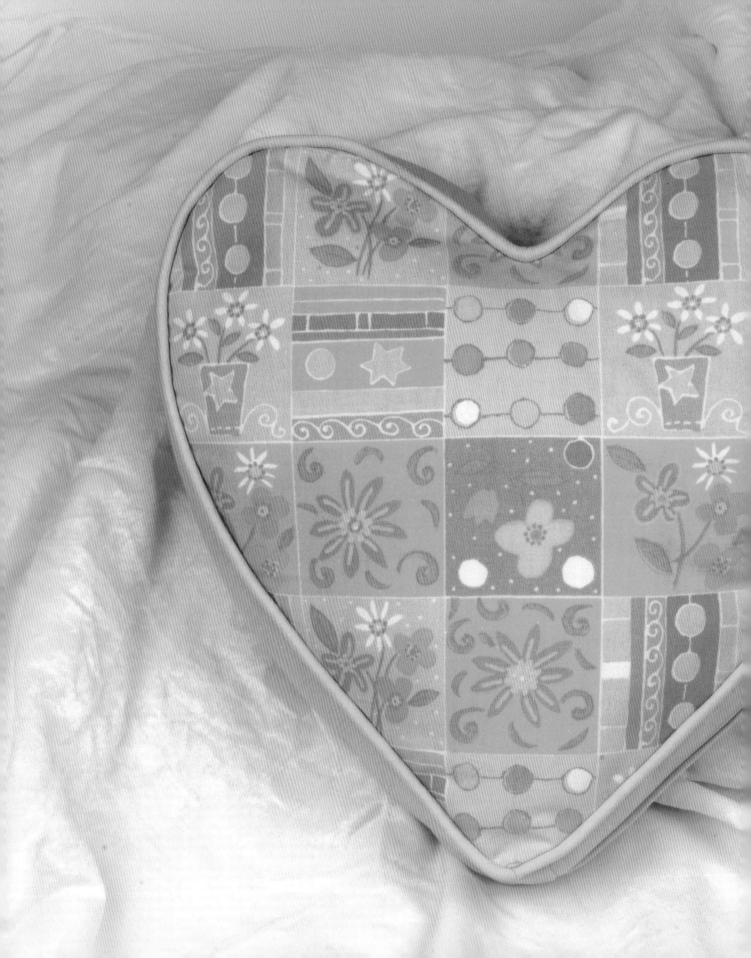

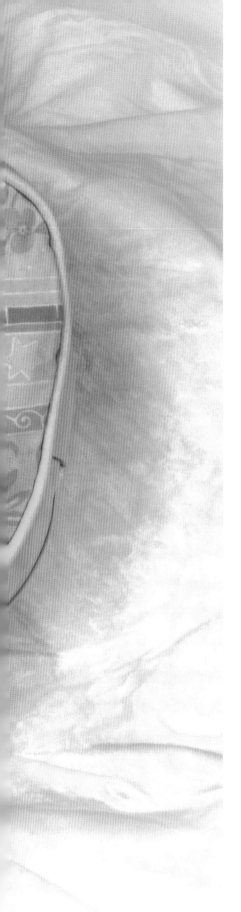

Heart's Delight

This pillow is sure to be the "heart" of your room. It can be made for Valentine's Day decorating or an everyday pillow, as we've shown here. We created this pillow for someone who loves a bit of whimsy in their room.

Materials:

- 1 yard of fabric or ½ yard of each of two contrasting fabrics like the sample shown
- 3 yards of welt cord
- Polyester stuffing or foam to fill and shape pillow (15"x15" finished size)
- 12" of zipper tape with slide
- Zipper foot
- Single welt foot

Cut:

Print the pattern pieces on your computer's printer from the CD-ROM. Tape all the sections together and lay the pattern on the fabric, lining up the arrow with the straight of grain. Cut out the heart following the instructions on the pattern piece. For the rise, cut one rectangle 3½"x50", and two rectangles 3½"x12". From the remaining fabric, make four yards of 2" bias for welt cord per the Making Continuous Bias instructions found on page 18.

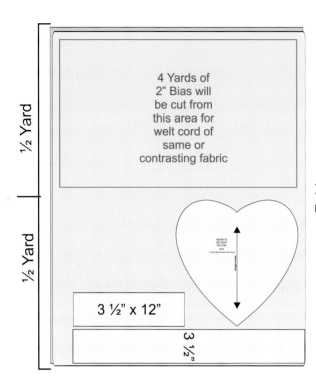

½ Yard

½ Yard

4 Yards of 2" Bias will be cut from this area for welt cord of same or contrasting fabric

HEART'S DELIGHT PILLOW Cut 2

3 ½" x 12"

3 ½"

1. Create the welting using the instructions for Making Welting found on page 20. With the right sides together, sew the welting along the edge of each heart section keeping the raw edges even. Splice the welting along one of the straight edges of the heart. Clip the welting lip along the curved edges to ease around the curves.

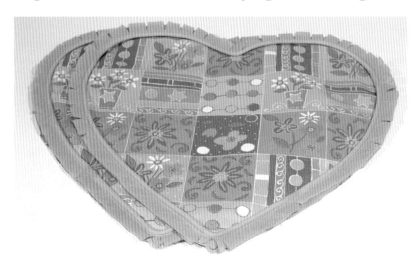

2. Snip the heart at the center top, as shown, to ease the seam allowance when turning right sides out.

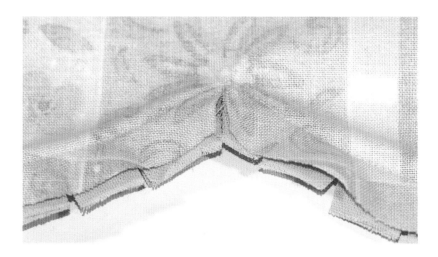

3. Fold the two short 3¹/₂"x 12" rectangles in half lengthwise, and press flat. Insert the zipper using the Rise Insertion instructions found on page 30. With right sides together, sew the long rectangle to the zipper placket on one end only. You will trim off the excess rise fabric, leaving a bit to fold over just before you finish sewing on the rise. This will help ease the other side and give protection to the zipper slide. Begin sewing the zipper placket along one of the straighter edges of the heart.

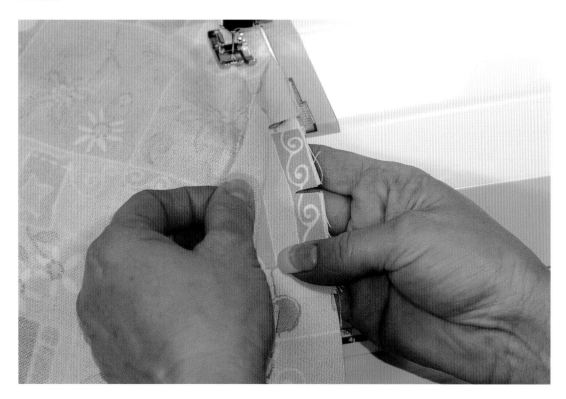

4. Sew until the two ends meet, like a wall. Stitch together and sew the other side to match. Notch the rise at the bottom point and center top, to help line up the top and bottom pieces.

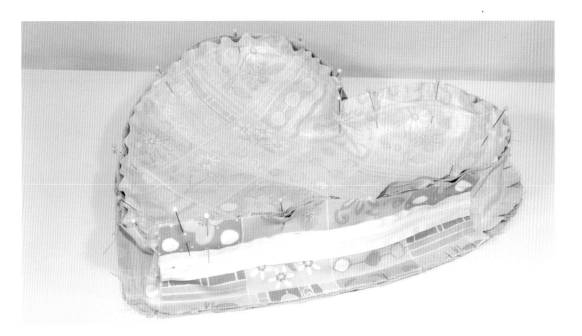

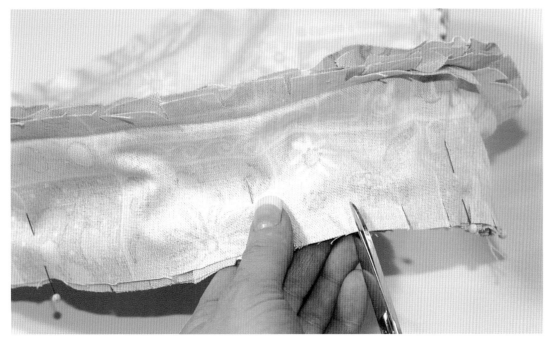

5. Pin the rise to the other side, matching at the center top and bottom of the pillow. Clip the rise on the curved edges of the pillow, to ease for turning.

6. Complete sewing the rise to the pillow and serge the seam allowances. Stuff with either foam or loose polyester stuffing.

Hero

Like many of you, Katie and I have loved ones and friends who are American heroes. Heroes come in many shapes and sizes. I personally think of my husband and daughter as being my heroes, as they have to live with me, and that's a lot for anyone to have to deal with! And of course, Katie is my other hero, as she had the courage to write this book with me and still remain my dear friend.

Materials:

- ¹/₂ yard of solid red fabric
- 17" zipper tape with slide
- June Tailor® Colorfast Sew-In Inkjet Fabric™ Sheets
- ¹/₂ yard black fabric for photo corners
- 16"-square pillow form
- Digital or scanned photo
- Zipper foot
- Single welt foot
- Optional: 24" pillow template

Embroidery Supplies:

- Hoop Size: 170mm x 100mm
- Stabilizer: Tear-away
- Contrasting 40wt rayon embroidery thread

Cut:

Let's begin with your digital photo. Crop and size the photo to fit your colorfast fabric sheet, or use an existing snapshot and enlarge the photo to fit. It's always advisable to print a practice copy on paper first to test your size and photo quality. Using the manufacturer's instructions, make a fabric print of the photo to be used.

From a single layer of red fabric, cut a 17" square for the pillow back. From the remaining 54" fabric, cut two strips to make the sashing for around the photo. These strips will vary in width based on the size of your photo. In general, if you cut your sashing 6" wide from the remaining fabric, you will have enough to trim and square up to 17" once the pillow top is pieced together.

From the black fabric, cut four 3½" squares; fold and press diagonally to form triangles. Print the photo corner pattern from the CD-ROM on your computer's printer.

1. Place the photo corner pattern on the folded fabric to mark the stitching lines for the notches. Stitch on the traced lines.

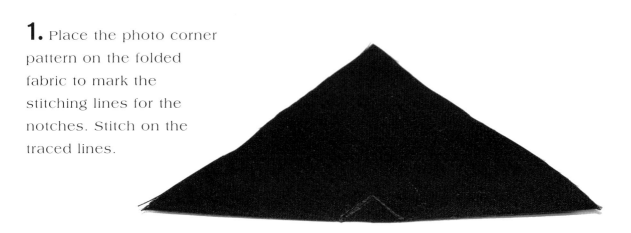

2. Clip all the way to the inside corner stitches.

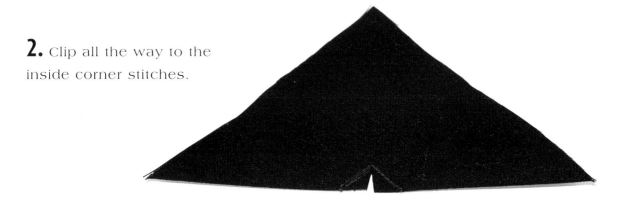

3. Turn right sides out and press flat.

4. Place each sewn photo corner on the corners of the photo and baste or pin into place. Fold the first sashing strip in half with 6" ends together. Cut the sashing strip in half at the fold. With right sides together, sew the top and bottom sashing pieces to the photo using a ¹/₂" seam allowance. Press the seam allowances away from the photo. Trim away any excess sashing even with your photo.

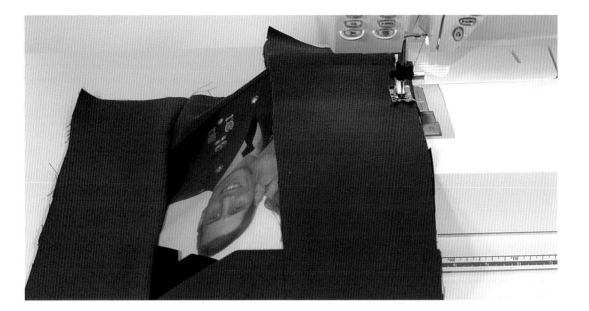

5. Next, cut the second sashing strip in the same manner as the first. With right sides together, sew the side sashing pieces to the pillow top and press the seam allowances away from the photo.

6. After all the sashing pieces are sewn, you may want to embellish with the "My Hero" embroidery found on the CD-ROM. Center the embroidery along the bottom sashing piece 1¼" from the bottom of the photo seam. You could even be creative by placing the embroidery at an angle in the corner. We give you full creative license on this one! This is a great personal pillow and is made extra-special by using your own memorable photos.

7. We chose to add a standard ¼" welt cord trim on our pillow. You may choose to trim your pillow by using a purchased trim or make your own. For instructions on making welt cord, please refer to the information found on page 20.

8. Prepare the pillow back using the instructions for the Placket Insertion, found on page 28, and insert your zipper. With right sides together, sew the pillow front to the pillow back. Trim the corners and turn right side out by opening the zipper and pulling the pillow through the zipper opening.

A Star is Born

Katie and I wanted to recognize all the men and women who serve in our armed forces, as well as their families here, preserving the home front, while they serve far away. To us, this star represents American freedom which none of us should take for granted.

Materials:

- 1 yard of white fabric
- 4 yards of purchased trim
  OR
  18" square of contrasting fabric for 4 yards of bias and 4 yards of welt cord
- 14" zipper tape with slide
- Zipper foot
- Edge stitching foot

Cut:

Copy the pattern on your computer's printer from the CD-ROM. Tape the pattern pieces together and lay out the star pattern as shown. You will need to cut four rectangular strips for the rise construction. Cut the following sizes: one 3"x54" (or the entire width of fabric), one 3"x7" (for ease on side of zipper placket), and two 3"x14" for the zipper placket.

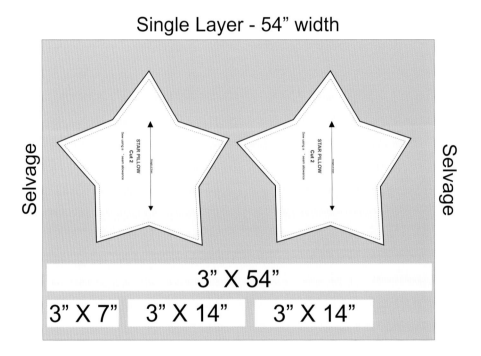

1. If you are making your own welting, please refer to both Making Welting and Making Continuous Bias instructions found on pages 20 and 18 respectively.

2. Sew the welting or purchased trim all the way around each side of the star. Begin sewing and splice the welting or trim at the bottom edge where the zipper will go. Be sure to clip into the inner corners of the star and clip the welting when sewing the inner and outer points, respectively.

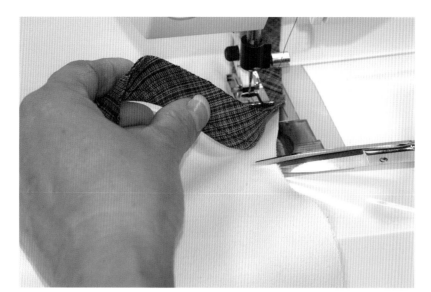

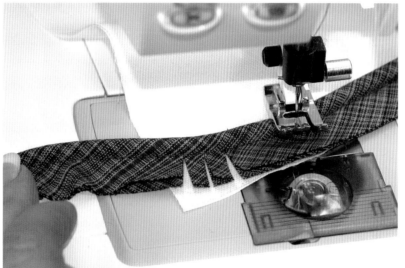

3. Fold each section of the zipper placket in half lengthwise and sew the zipper in place according to the instructions for the Rise Insertion found on page 30.

4. Sew the two rise pieces (3"x7" and 3"x54") end to end, right sides together, to make one long strip. Sew the rise to the zipper placket, end to end, and sew to the pillow top. If necessary, review the Rise Insertion instructions for zipper insertion techniques. Fold the rise over at each end of the zipper placket to create ease when sewing on the other side.

5. Fold the rise at each star point, and snip ¼" to mark star point placement for the other side of the pillow.

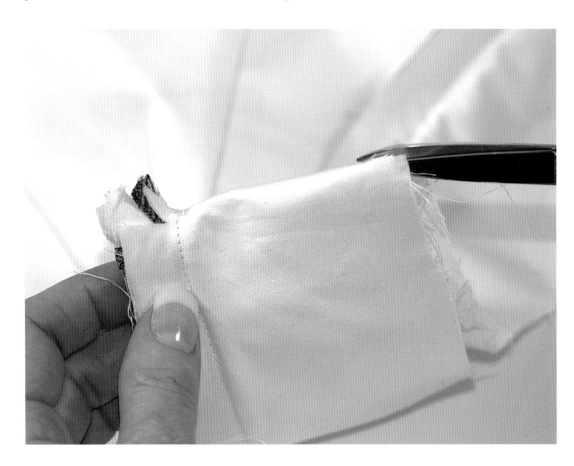

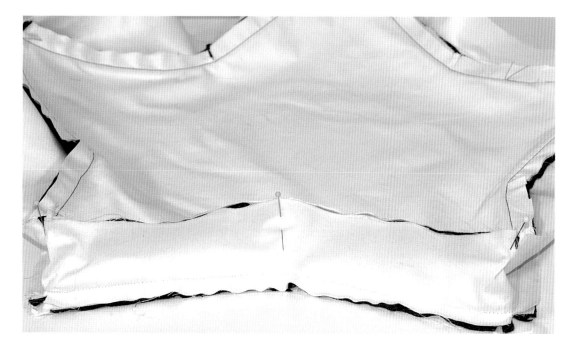

6. Starting at one end of the zipper placket, begin sewing the rise to the pillow top, sewing the zipper section last. Adjust the folds for ease and complete by sewing the zipper section of the rise.

7. Inspect all the corners to make sure they've been sewn out correctly. Finish by serging all the seam allowances.

Just
Dreamy

Rhubarb Custard Pie

This recipe came from Diane Shealy-Murphy, a Damour certified instructor. She makes the pie with coconut but, with all the garden-fresh rhubarb we have, this is how we often enjoy it!

4 eggs
1 cup sugar
1 cup flour
2 teaspoons vanilla
1 cup milk
1 stick of butter
1$\frac{1}{2}$ cups chopped raw unpeeled rhubarb

Preheat oven to 350°.

Put all ingredients except for rhubarb into a blender and blend until smooth. Pour into a greased pie plate and add rhubarb. The flour and butter will magically find each other, forming their own crust! Bake for 45 to 50 minutes. Serves 8.

Note: You may substitute other fruit or coconut for rhubarb.

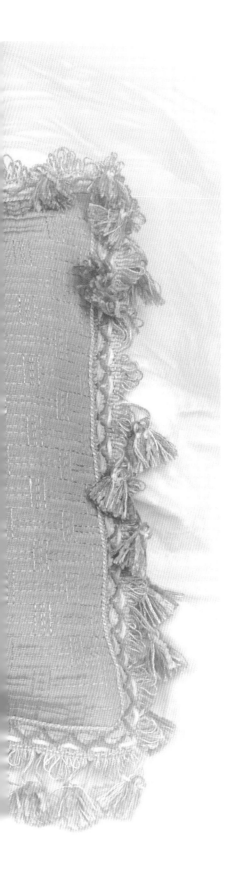

Quilted Celtic Elegance

When Katie and I found a photo of a quilted neckroll in one of our home decorating magazines, we were both excited about the idea of re-creating a similar quilted design in the Celtic flavor in the embroidery hoop. I'd like to take some of the credit on this project, but really, it was all Katie. All I did was sew it together and add the trim!

Materials:

- ³/₄ yard of solid fabric for center section, bias welt, and back
- ¹/₂ yard of solid fabric for side sections
- ¹/₂ yard of batting for side sections
- 32" of welt cord for double welt (Optional: Or try flat braid or gimp over the seam to "dress it up" if you don't own a double welt foot.)
- 1 yard of braid or tassel trim
- Zipper foot
- Double welt foot
- Optional: Sulky® KK2000 basting spray
- 21" zipper tape with slide
- 14" x 20" pillow form

Embroidery Supplies:

- Hoop Size: 360mm x 150mm Mega Hoop for quilted edge; 240mm x 150mm for center section
- Stabilizer: Sulky® Cut-Away Plus™
- Two coordinating 40wt rayon embroidery threads, light and dark

Cut:

From the center fabric, cut a 12"x17" rectangle and two 16"x2½" bias pieces for the double welting. Cut two 10"x18" rectangles for the side sections from the fabric and the batting.

1. First, hoop your stabilizer only. Lay one 10"x18" batting and one side section rectangle on top of the hooped stabilizer. If your machine has a "baste in the hoop" function (FIX), this is a great opportunity to use it. It will keep the layers together nicely for stitching the embroidery. If you don't have a FIX function, use Sulky® KK2000 to spray-baste the layers together before laying them on top of the hooped stabilizer. If there is any design in the fabric, make sure you squareup the fabric in the hoop so the embroidery is not sewn crooked. You will embroider the two side sections to the batting pieces before trimming the sections to size.

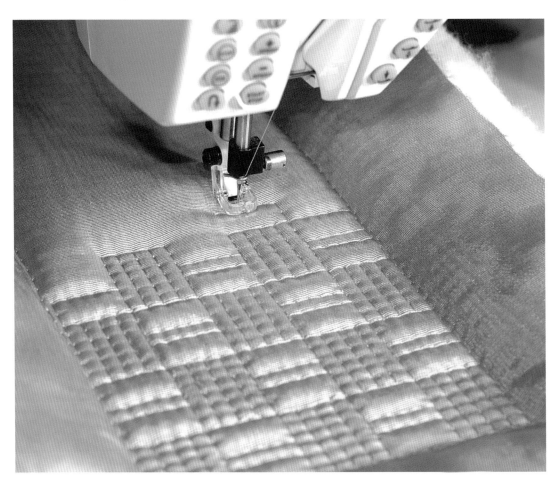

2. Next, embroider the pillow center by hooping both the center fabric and cut-away stabilizer to help keep the satin stitches beautiful. Center the Quilted Celtic Elegance pillow embroidery found on the CD-ROM in the center of the solid 12"x17" piece of fabric. Use your coordinating thread to stitch out the embroidery.

3. Trim the center pillow panel to 10"x15", making sure to trim evenly from all sides to keep the embroidery design centered.

4. Baste around the quilted side sections about 3/8" from the edge of the embroidered stitching.

5. Trim 1/2" away from the edge of the basting stitches. If necessary, trim each side section to 7"x15". Sew the three pillow top sections together, right sides together, along the 15" edges. Press the seams flat and toward the center section.

6. Using the directions beginning on page 23 for making double welting using the bias strips and the welt cord, lay the double welting (or flat trim) over the seams, as shown, and stitch down

the center of the double welt. Using a stiletto and a double welt foot while you're sewing really helps to hold the trim in place.

7. Measure the pillow front to make sure it measures 21"x15". Trim equally on all sides, if necessary, to this measurement. After sizing the pillow front, add the tassel trim. Sew the trim on as shown, starting at a bottom corner and stitching along the inside edge. Miter at the corners, but only sew the trim down on the inside edge. You will sew down the miter later at its 45° angle once all the trim is attached.

8. To stitch the last corner, fold the trim under at a 45° angle as shown, and complete the stitching along the inside edge.

9. Before sewing the back of the pillow to the front, flip the loose edge of the trim toward the inside of the pillow and pin to hold temporarily.

10. Insert the zipper using the Bottom Edge Insertion technique found on page 32. After the zipper has been sewn on each side and married together with the slide, pin the remaining sides together being sure not to catch the trim in your stitching. Serge the seam allowances and turn pillow right side out through the open zipper. After the pillow is turned right side out, hand- or machine-stitch the miters at each corner to secure them flat to the pillow top. Insert the pillow form.

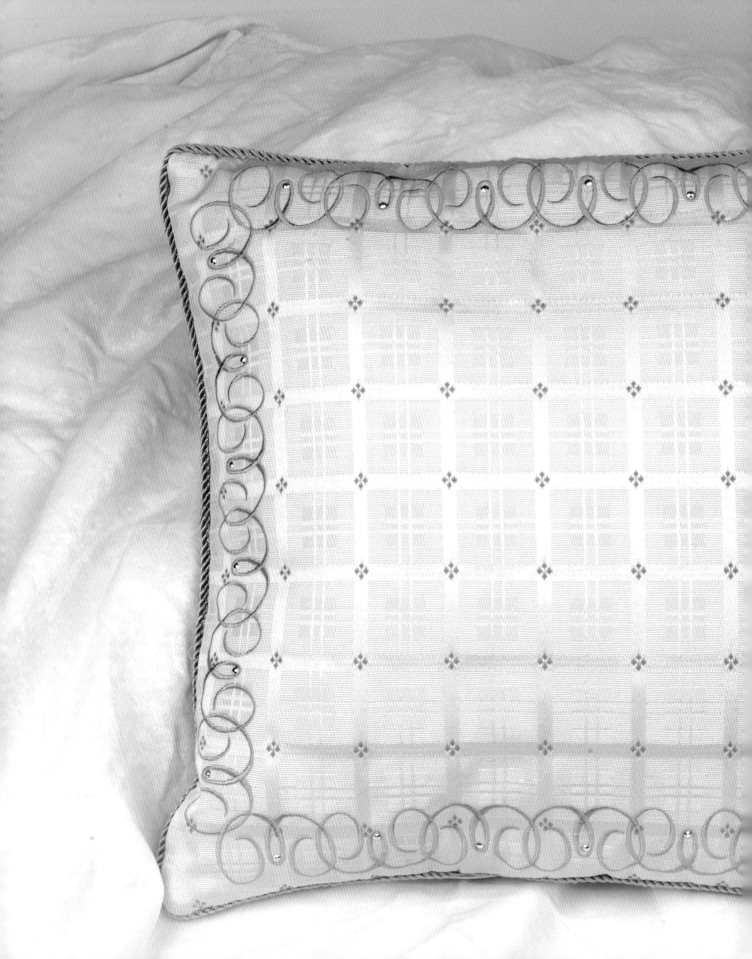

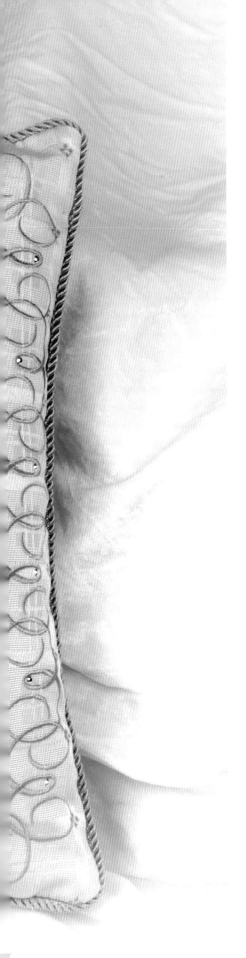

Katie's Gone Loopy!

Katie had so much fun designing this endless embroidery design, that we decided she had gone "loopy"! Katie wanted the design to be just right. She wanted an endless loop design simple and elegant enough to be embroidered on anything but also make a 90° pivot, too!

Materials:

- ⅝ yard of home decorating fabric
- 19" zipper tape with slide
- 2⅛ yards of twisted cord or other trim
- 18" square pillow form
- Narrow zipper foot for twisted cord
- Regular zipper foot for zipper insertion
- Water- or air-soluble marker
- Crystals and L'orna® Decorative Touch™ Wand

Embroidery Supplies:

- Hoop Size: 170mm x 100mm Endless Embroidery Hoop
- Stabilizer: Sulky® Totally Stable™ Iron-on Tear-Away Stabilizer or Sulky® KK2000 basting spray
- Coordinating 40wt rayon embroidery thread

JUST DREAMY

Cut:

Cut one 20" square for the pillow front. The Endless Embroidery hoop will be used to embroider a design on this piece and then trimmed to 19" after embroidering. Cut a 19" square for the pillow back and a 2"x19" piece for the zipper placket.

1. Begin by using an iron-on stabilizer, such as Sulky® Totally Stable™, or use Sulky® KK2000 to temporarily adhere the stabilizer to the back of your 20" square along the edges. You will apply the stabilizer matching the edges with the fabric as the edge will help you guide your fabric through the embroidery hoop.

2. Mark a dot with a water- or air-soluble marker 7" down from the top and 3½" in from one edge of the fabric square as shown on the illustration. This point marks the center of the embroidery hoop. Before you begin the embroidery, center the dot in the hoop by lowering your needle on the drawn mark. Align the fabric with the hoop guide and close the embroidery hoop. Note: The hoop's guide will be almost all the way to the right. Adjust hoop guide as necessary. This guide may be adjusted when we use the pivot jump stitch. Begin your embroidery and complete two full designs before getting ready to pivot the pillow top.

Hint: On the pillow top, draw a line 5" from the edge all the way around with invisible marker or chalk liner. This line will help you keep the fabric visually straight in the hoop, along with the fabric hoop guide. I sometimes draw a line at 3" around also, as I'm a visual sewer; it helps me be more accurate. It also makes it easier to spot check and measure the distance of the lines from the edge of the inside hoop for even more accuracy!

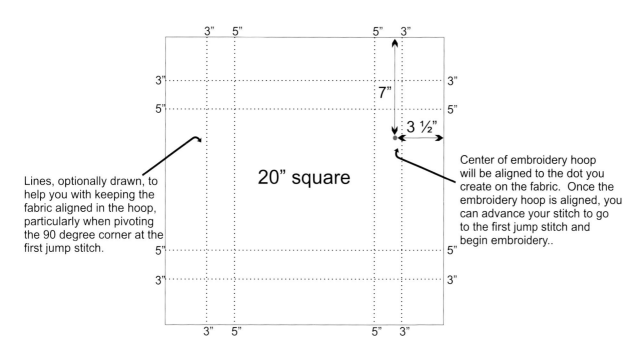

Lines, optionally drawn, to help you with keeping the fabric aligned in the hoop, particularly when pivoting the 90 degree corner at the first jump stitch.

20" square

Center of embroidery hoop will be aligned to the dot you create on the fabric. Once the embroidery hoop is aligned, you can advance your stitch to go to the first jump stitch and begin embroidery..

3. As the first embroidery design completes, it will finish with two jump stitches. A stop command has also been added to the design so you can use a water- or air-soluble marker to mark the jump stitches, if desired. The first jump stitch is used for the 90° pivot, and the second jump stitch is used for placing the fabric for continuous, straight line embroidery. For this first design repeat, align your needle to the second jump stitch position after advancing your needle position one stitch.

4. The next stitch out needs to use the first jump stitch needle position in order to make the design pivot correctly. Having the 5" and 3" lines drawn around the pillow top will help you make an exact 90° turn. After you advance your stitch to move to the first jump stitch position, align your needle with the first jump stitch position. Before closing the hoop, pivot the 20" square 90°. You can measure from the inside left edge of the hoop to the drawn line(s). Making the measurements equal at the top and bottom of the loops will guarantee that you have pivoted the corner at 90°. Continue embroidering two stitch-outs on each side of the pillow top, pivoting after the second stitch-out.

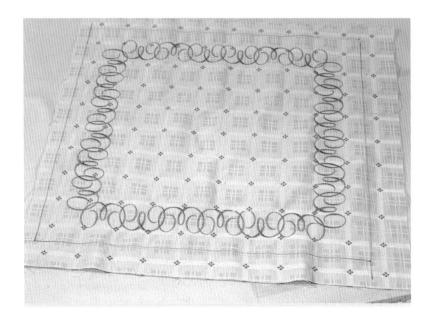

5. After completing the entire embroidery, press the fabric and trim the square to 19". Using the pillow template can quickly help you square up your pillow top!

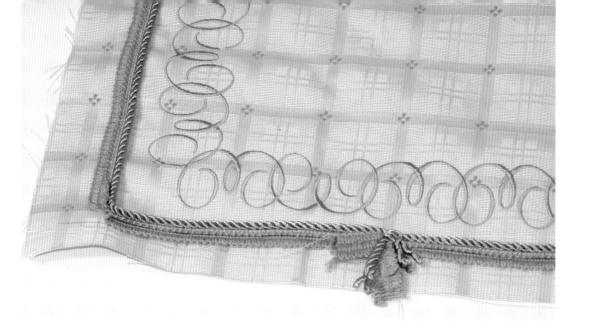

6. Sew the twisted cord trim along the edges of the 19" pillow top, using the basic instructions for Inserting Twisted Cord found on page 26. Feel free to be creative with your trims—select purchased trims or some made by yourself. Trim away any excess fabric leaving a ½" seam for attaching the pillow back.

7. Insert the zipper into the back using the instructions found on page 28 for Placket Insertion.

8. Once the zipper was inserted, we added crystals with the L'orna® Decorative Touch™ Wand to various parts of the embroidery design to spice things up a bit.

9. Insert pillow form.

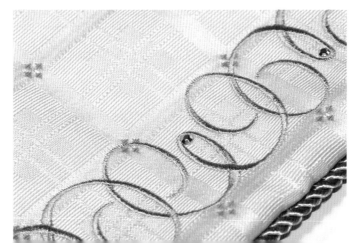

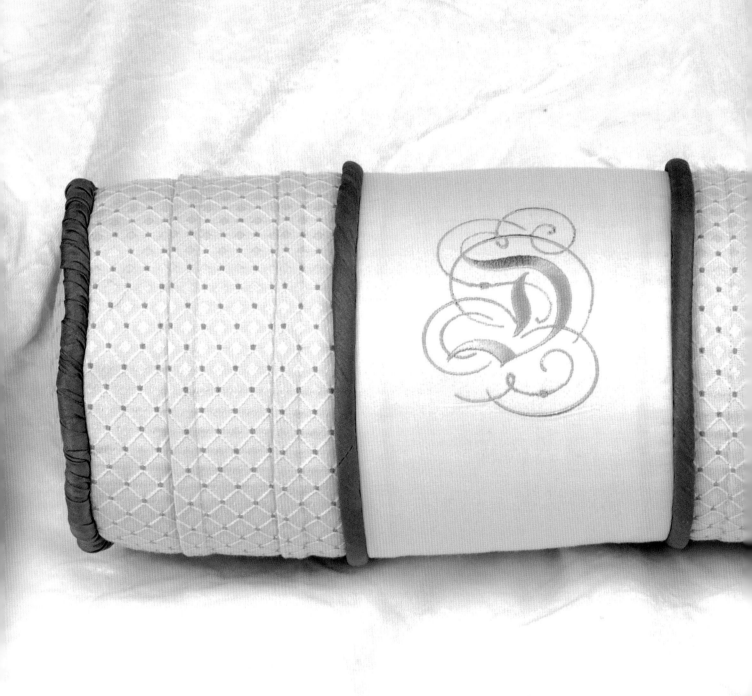

Mono-grammed Neckroll

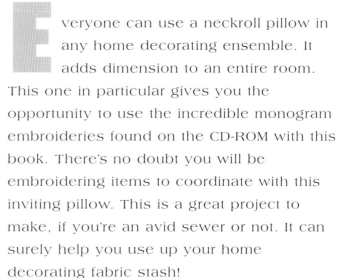

Everyone can use a neckroll pillow in any home decorating ensemble. It adds dimension to an entire room. This one in particular gives you the opportunity to use the incredible monogram embroideries found on the CD-ROM with this book. There's no doubt you will be embroidering items to coordinate with this inviting pillow. This is a great project to make, if you're an avid sewer or not. It can surely help you use up your home decorating fabric stash!

Materials:

- ¼ yard of fabric for center section
- ½ yard of fabric for the side and end sections
- ⅓ yard of coordinating fabric to make welting and shirred welting
- 2½ yards of ⅜" welt cord
- ½ yard of zipper tape with slide
- 6"x14" neckroll pillow form or enough loose batting to fill
- Ruffler attachment
- Edge stitching foot
- Narrow zipper foot

Embroidery Supplies:

- Hoop Size: 100mm x 100mm hoop
- Stabilizer: Sulky® Cut-Away Plus™ stabilizer or Sulky® Totally Stable™ Iron-on Tear-Away Stabilizer
- Coordinating 40wt rayon embroidery thread

JUST DREAMY

Cut:

Cut an 8"x24" rectangle of fabric for the center section to embroider your monogram. Use one of the monogram embroideries on the CD-ROM, or use one of your own. Center the embroidery design, 7" up from the bottom. If you do not own an embroidery machine, you may choose to hand embroider a monogram, or purchase one of the many iron-on monogram embroideries available at your local fabric store.

From the side fabric, cut two 10"x22" pieces and two 7" circles using the pattern found on the CD-ROM.

Center Fabric
Embroidery Layout
8"

24"

4"

7"

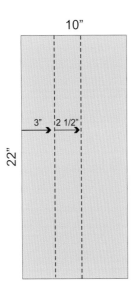

10"

22"

3" 2 1/2"

1. On the wrong side, mark two lines 2 1/2" apart starting 3" from the long edge.

2. With wrong sides together, press on each mark and sew a 1/2" tuck along the folded edge.

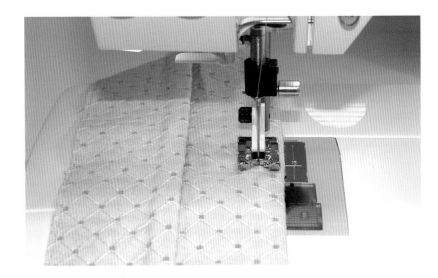

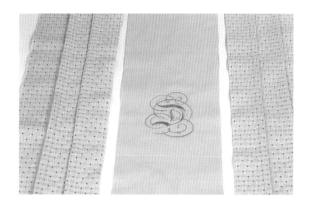

3. Press tucks toward the outside edge.

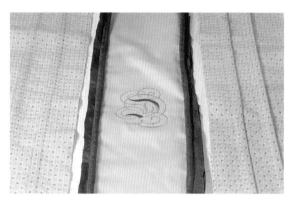

4. To insert the welt cord, refer to Making Welting found on page 20. Trim the center embroidered section to 6" wide. Sew the welt cord using the single welt foot along each long edge of the center section, as shown.

5. Sew each tucked side section to the center section to create a larger rectangle. Trim from both sides evenly to 15" wide by 19" long. Cut a 15" length of zipper tape and separate into two pieces. With right sides together, sew one side of the zipper tape to the bottom edge, as shown. Sew the other side of the zipper tape to the top edge in the same manner.

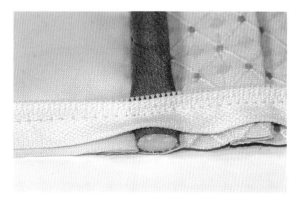

JUST DREAMY

6. Insert the zipper slide and run back and forth two times so the pillow is married together and both zipper ends are closed. Leave the zipper slide in the middle of the zipper to open and turn right side out when the pillow is completed.

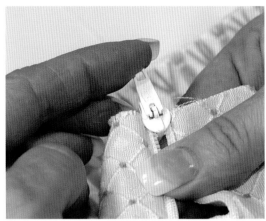

7. Cut 5 yards of 2 1/2" bias. Run each edge of bias through the ruffler to make ruching. Wrap the ruching around the welt cord and sew the edges together. Review the instructions for Shirred Welting found on page 25 for more detailed photos. Sew the ruched welting to each of the 7" circles making sure right sides are together and raw edges are even. Splice the ends by removing the stitches on one end and wrapping the fabric over the other end; stitch to hold.

8. To find the center on each side, fold the pillow body in half and notch at the zipper placket to mark the center bottom, then notch the center top and center sides. Do the same with the round pillow ends, notching at the center top, bottom, and sides.

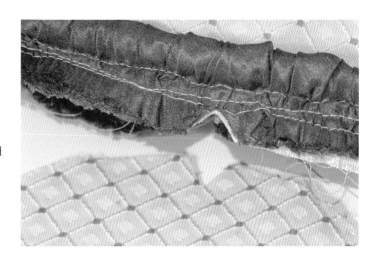

9. Match the notches on the round ends to the pillow body and pin together, as shown.

10. Stitch around the end with a narrow zipper foot, using the previous stitching lines on the shirred welting as your guide. Adjust your needle position so the stitching is as close to the welt as possible. Serge the seam allowances to finish. Turn right side out and stuff with the pillow form or batting.

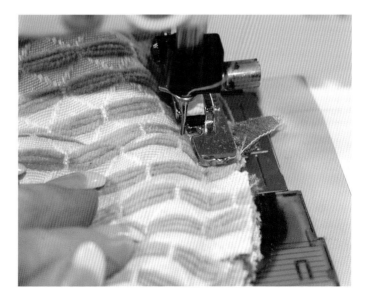

It's A Guy Thing

Cream of
Wild Rice Soup

Katie lives in Minnesota, and you can't go anywhere without being able to get a great bowl of Minnesota Wild Rice Soup. Here's one of Katie's favorites, because it's easy and tasty, too!

1 bunch of celery, chopped
1 large onion, chopped
2 quarts chicken stock or broth
4 to 6 cups chicken or turkey, chopped
1 pound of wild rice, steamed
1 teaspoon sage or poultry seasoning
1 quart of Half and Half
1 large jar of Cheese Whiz
Two 10-ounce cans of cream of celery soup
One 50-ounce cream of mushroom soup

In a skillet, saute the celery and onion. Add to broth and chicken in a stock pot. Simmer on low and add wild rice and seasoning. Add Half and Half, Cheese Whiz, and creamed soups at the very end. This soup freezes well.

Endless Leaves

This project uses the Husqvarna Viking Endless Embroidery Hoop, which allows you to rehoop your fabric quickly and easily, creating an endless design. If you don't have an endless hoop, use a 100mm x 170mm hoop, and rehoop as needed. The jump stitches in the design will help you rehoop with greater accuracy! The design, which cascades over the top of the pillow, can also be used on the front of a larger pillow or bed sham.

This embroidery design is unique in that it contains two jump stitches for the Endless Embroidery Hoop, instead of the standard single jump stitch. One jump stitch is used to align the continuous designs and a second jump stitch is used for alignment on a 90° corner. Stop commands are also included at the jump stitch locations so you can use an invisible marker to mark the needle positions, if desired. Now how easy is that?

Materials:

- 17"x 25½" of fabric for background section
- 13"x18½" of coordinating fabric for embroidery
- 17" of zipper tape with slide
- 12"x16" pillow form
- Zipper foot
- Edge joining foot
- Air-soluble marker or chalk liner

Embroidery Supplies:

- Hoop Size: 170mm x 100mm Endless Embroidery Hoop
- Stabilizer: Sulky® Totally Stable™ Iron-on Tear-Away Stabilizer
- 30 wt Sulky® Blendable thread

1. To embroider the coordinating fabric with the leaves, draw a line across the 13" side 5¼" down from the top edge. Hoop your stabilized fabric and place the line across the center position markings in the Endless Hoop. This will get you started in the correct position for the sewing the design and allow enough room for trimming when the fabric in completely embroidered. Place the adjustable embroidery guide 3⅜" from the needle. Lay the fabric next to the guide and close the embroidery hoop. Begin stitching.

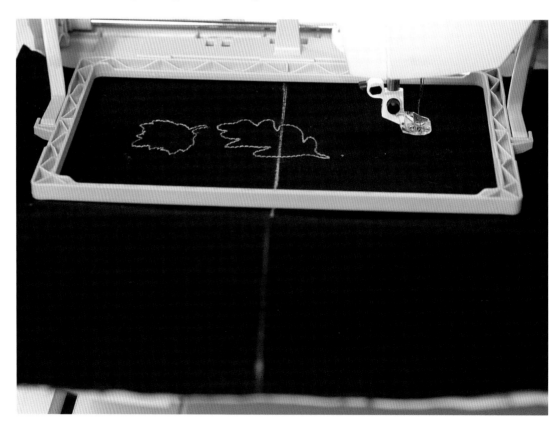

2. When the first embroidery is finished, it will stop at the first jump stitch. Either continue embroidering, or take your marking pen and mark the position of this first jump stitch. (You may need to lower your needle to get the exact location.) The first jump stitch is used if you want to continue the embroidery design in a straight line, which you will do at this point. You will use this jump stitch to complete the first side of this embroidery project.

3. After the second embroidery segment is completed, stitch through the first jump stitch. At the second stop, take your marker and mark the jump stitch position for the pivoting point. Again, you may need to lower your needle to get the exact position. Continue using the same techniques as you do when you use the endless hoop, but pivot your fabric 90° before continuing the embroidery. Align the second jump stitch after pivoting, and embroider one complete design before using the second jump stitch to pivot and go up the other side. (Don't forget to advance your embroidery design before aligning to the jump stitch. Ask me how I know!) When your embroidery is finished, it will be a continuous rectangle of embroidery, perfectly spaced and ready to attach to the background fabric!

4. Draw lines 1" from the outside and inside edges of the embroidered design.

5. Center the embroidered section over the background fabric, pinning it in place. To do this easily, snip a small notch in the center of the background fabric and embroidered fabric to center the pieces. When placing a notch in the embroidered section, be sure to notch after matching the drawn lines rather than the edge of the fabric. This will give you more accuracy when centering.

6. Stitch a straight line over the drawn lines to attach the embroidered section to the background fabric. Trim away all excess fabric close to the outer stitching line. Remove the fabric from inside the rectangle along the line.

7. Satin-stitch over the trimmed edges on both the inside and outside of the embroidered piece. Note: If your sewing machine has a mitered satin stitch, you may want to use it to create a mitered frame at the corners around the embroidery. To use the mitered satin stitch, begin with a 6mm satin stitch. Sew all the way to the corner, ending with the needle positioned on the right side. Press the mitered satin stitch from your stitch menu, pivot, and begin stitching over the wide satin stitching. The mitered satin stitching will begin narrow and get wider to match the edge of the other stitching.

8. Press the two bottom edges up ½" for the zipper. Sew one side to each side of the zipper tape and add the slide. Follow the instructions on page 32 for the Bottom Edge Insertion zipper application. With right sides together, stitch both ends closed. Serge or zigzag the seam allowances and turn right side out. Fill with the pillow form.

Tassels Abound

We are often trimming the corners of our pillows to prevent "dog-ears". We thought it would be fun to actually make a pillow with extreme dog-ears, so here it is! This pillow will be man's best friend!

Materials:

- ½ yard of fabric
- 5" square of coordinating fabric for center monogram
- 2½ yards of twisted cord with lip
- 18" zipper tape with slide
- Four tassels
- Narrow zipper foot
- Double welting foot or edge joining foot
- Air-soluble marker or chalk liner

Embroidery Supplies:

- Hoop Size: 100mm x 100mm hoop for monogram
- Stabilizer: Sulky® Totally Stable™ Iron-on Tear-Away Stabilizer
- Coordinating 40wt rayon embroidery thread

Cut:

Cut out the pillow top and back using the pattern you printed off the CD-ROM, matching any pattern in your fabric.

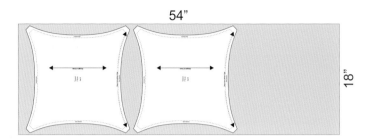

1. Using a zipper foot and starting in the center of the bottom edge of the pillow top, begin sewing the twisted cord on the pillow leaving 1$^1/_2$" not sewn so that you can splice the cord together when stitched all around. Clip into the lip of the twisted cord at each corner, before sewing it to the corner.

Hint: Keep the ends of twisted cord taped to prevent ravelling and fraying.

2. To splice the trim, sew until the two ends butt up to each other and create a "wall".

3. Remove the stitching from the lip and twisted cord on each end of the cord.

4. Overlap the cord in the direction of the twist.

5. Sew the cord overlap in place using the zipper foot. Note: To create a smooth splice, you may need to sew the cording in the opposite direction, as well as mirror-image your needle position so you are sewing in the direction of the twist. The result is a virtually hidden splice!

6. If you choose to add an appliquéd monogram, embroider the monogram in the center of the 5" square of fabric. (We used a scrap from the ottoman project on pages 100-105, which had 4" squares in the fabric.) Draw a 4" square around your monogram for placement of the twisted cord.

7. Use the remaining twisted cord to edge the appliquéd piece. Sew the twisted cord on the drawn line as shown, making sure to clip as you turn the corners. Splice the twisted cord according to the instructions above.

8. Trim the corners off the twisted cord lip as shown. Press to the inside, so the twisted cord is at the edge.

9. Center the appliqué on the pillow top and stitch-in-the-ditch close to the twisted cord. Move your needle position as necessary.

10. Before sewing the pillow top to the back, add the zipper following the instructions found on page 32 for the Bottom Edge Insertion technique. Press under ½" on each bottom edge. Separate the zipper tape, and sew one side to each bottom edge of the pillow top and back.

11. You are now ready to sew the pillow back to the pillow top and insert the tassels. Pin a tassel at each corner with the tassel body to the inside. Use your stiletto to keep all the pieces in place as you sew the top to the back.

12. Clip the curved edges and serge the seam allowances. Turn right side out and stuff.

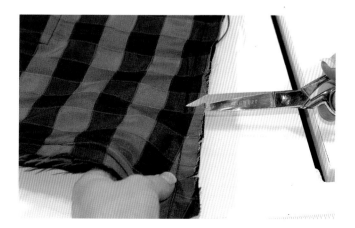

Convertible
Ottoman

T his is a fun contemporary design that uses three floor cushions, stacked on a base which converts into an ottoman. That's why we call it a "convertible"! This project wasn't completed even an hour, when Pam's calico cat decided it would be the perfect place to take a nap. We chose to make the cushions without a welt cord edge for a cleaner look.

Materials:

- 20"x24" piece of 3/4" plywood
- Four 2" diameter castors
- 1½ yards of fabric for the base and one cushion
- 2½ yards of coordinating fabric for two cushions
- 60"x24"x4" piece of foam
- 5 yards of 27"-wide bonded upholstery Dacron batting
- Spray adhesive
- Staple gun with ½" staples
- 90" of zipper tape and 3 slides
- 3/4 yard of cambric or muslin to cover wood base bottom
- Zipper foot
- Fasturn™ tool
- Optional: 2½ yards of bullion trim

Cut:

Cut the fabric for two matching cushions: four 21"x25" for cushions and six 4"x54" for the rise. For the remaining cushion and base, cut two 21"x25" for the cushion, three 4"x54" for the rise, and one 27"x31" for the base.

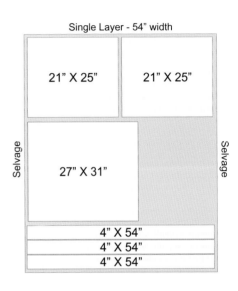

1. Pulling the base fabric taut, staple onto wood base as shown. You may want to cover the exposed wood on the bottom with cambric, muslin, or lining.

2. Mount each castor approximately 2" in from the corners, as shown.

3. If you choose to add bullion trim, staple or glue it onto the ottoman base edge now.

4. Use decorative tacks to secure the trim permanently. Here's your chance to make this ottoman your own!

5. If you would like to add the boxed corner ties, cut bias strips 2"x6" from the remaining cushion fabric. You can choose to cut ties out of the same or coordinating fabric, as we have done. Sew, right sides together, along the entire length of each strip. Turn right side out by using a Fasturn® tool. Pin a tie to each corner of the pillow top and bottom, on the right side.

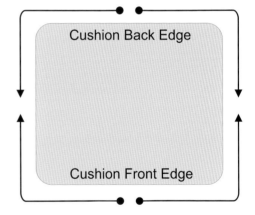

Cushion Back Edge

Cushion Front Edge

6. Make zipper rises using the instructions found on page 30 for the Rise Insertion. Begin sewing the zipper rise in the center back, sewing from the center out on each side.

7. Then using the front rise section, begin with the center of the rise and the center of the cushion front. Cut a small notch or mark with a pin, the centers of the cushion sections and rises to mark your starting points for sewing. Sew from the center out. Sew the zipper rise to the front rise at the sides where they meet.

8. After sewing the rise to one side of the cushion, notch the rise at the corners. Match all the corners of the next cushion piece to the notches in the rise. Pin the cushion section in place. Complete by sewing the remaining side according to the diagram on the previous page. Refer to the zipper Rise Insertion instructions found on page 30 to learn how to add the appropriate ease to the cushions. Turn right side out and inspect for a smooth seam before serging the seam allowances.

9. Cut the foam the finished dimension of your cushion and wrap with Dacron batting to give the cushion the soft loft you see in this photo. Whipstitch or spray-glue the Dacron batting to the foam.

10. Tie the cushion ties together and knot the ends, as shown. Trim off any excess bias.

Special time

Pam's Grandmother's Baked Beans

e all have someone, who for one reason or another, has shaped our lives more than anyone else. In my life, so many wonderful relatives, in-laws, and friends have blessed me, but if I had to single out one person as being life altering for me, she would have to be my Grandma Rabideau. Grandma was only 35 when I was born, just a young girl herself. She taught me about the birds and the bees, how to milk cows, and most importantly, she was my inspiration to sew. For as long at I can remember, she had an old blue straight-stitch sewing machine set up in her bedroom. I often tell stories of my "sewing fairy" that I believe is Grandma. Before she died peacefully in my arms, she shared with me some cherished family recipes that I continue to make for my family. Christmas, Easter, and other special family gatherings are not complete without "the beans".

The quantities are approximate, because when Grandma cooked, we never measured anything. Add each ingredient to taste, and if they don't turn out right, try again. Even as I write this, my beans are soaking for tomorrow's christening ceremony for our first great-niece.

One small bag of navy beans
2 tablespoons baking soda
1 to 1½ cups sugar
1 tablespoon dried mustard
Salt and pepper to taste
Bacon to cover top

Wash and sort the beans, throwing out any discolored ones. For best results, soak overnight in water with about 2 tablespoons of baking soda. (This helps eliminate gastric activity on the part of the consumer!) If you are cooking the beans right away, put them on the stove on low heat with lots of water, add the baking soda, and simmer until the water turns very yellow. Rinse the beans in HOT water, until the water runs clear. Return the beans to the stove, with enough water to cover. Continue to simmer over low heat until beans are tender. You may need to add a small amount of water to keep the beans from sticking, but try to keep water amount to a minimum.

After beans are tender, remove from heat and add sugar (about 1½ cups) until beans are quite sweet. You need to make them sweeter than desired, because as they bake, the beans will absorb the sugar so they won't be as sweet after baking. Add the dry mustard, salt and pepper, and stir to mix. Put into baking dish. Lay strips of bacon over top, covering the top, and bake at 350° for about one hour, or until the beans aren't runny and the bacon is browned.

Katie's Grandmother's Pistachio Cake

remember my Grandma Trevis making this cake often when I was a little girl. She always seemed to have some on hand when she was teaching me to hand-embroider! The pistachio green color of this cake always makes it a festive event, whenever you need something sweet. My grandmother was also my inspiration for sewing. Thanks Granny!

1 package white cake mix
1 package pistachio pudding mix
4 eggs
½ cup vegetable oil
½ cup fresh orange juice
½ cup water
¾ cup Hershey's Chocolate Syrup

Put everything, except the chocolate syrup, into a bowl and beat well. Grease and flour a cake pan. Pour about ⅔ of the batter into the pan. In the remaining batter, add the Hershey's syrup and beat well. Pour over the top of the green batter. Bake in a 350° oven for 25-30 minutes. (Granny said it was done when the toothpick you poked in came out clean!)

For a fun variation, bake the batter in flat-bottom ice cream cones! Place the cones in a muffin pan, fill ½ full with green batter, and put the chocolate batter on top of that, until it's about 1" from the top. Bake 25-30 minutes or until the toothpick comes out clean! Cool and frost! Kids of all ages will love this one!

Pam's Poinsettia

e thought about categorizing our pillows in this book under beginner, intermediate, and advanced. This pillow falls under "you've got to be kidding"! Perhaps that was because this pillow appeared it would take the longest to design and stitch out. I think it's one of our favorites. Of course you can make it with the traditional red with green leaves, or make it all one color. Whatever you decide, have fun with this one!

Materials:

- ¹/₂ yard of poinsettia flower fabric
- ¹/₄ yard of fabric for leaves
- ¹/₂ yard of fabric for pillow body
- 17" of zipper tape with slide
- 27" square of quilt batting
- Thread to match fabric
- 30 or 40wt rayon, variegated, or blendable embroidery thread for topstitching
- Dritz® button cover kit, size 60
- Crystals or Gold Rhine Studs and L'orna® Decorative Touch™ Wand
- Jeans or denim needle, size 90
- 16"-square pillow form
- Zipper foot
- Edge joining foot
- Air-soluble marker
- Optional: quilter's basting gun with T-tags

Cut:

Print out the patterns on your computer's printer from the CD-ROM. Note: If you print on heavier card stock, it's easier to trace around the patterns.

Trace four of each of the pattern pieces on the fabric as shown, layering two layers of fabric, right sides together, and a layer of batting on the bottom. Note: For the batting to end up on the inside when turned, it must start on the outside when stitched. Leave at least ½" between pieces, as the tracing line will also be your stitching line through all layers. Use the remaining flower fabric to make the covered button for the flower center.

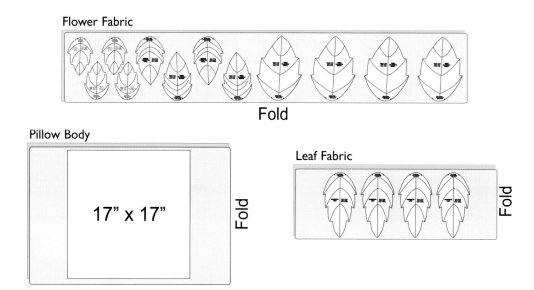

Flower Fabric

Fold

Pillow Body

17" x 17"

Fold

Leaf Fabric

Fold

1. Beginning at the bottom of the leaf or petal, sew on the traced lines. Remember, you have two layers of fabric, right sides together, and a layer of batting on the bottom. Leave the bottom open between the marks on the pattern for turning.

2. It's easier to stitch around all the traced lines before cutting the pieces apart.

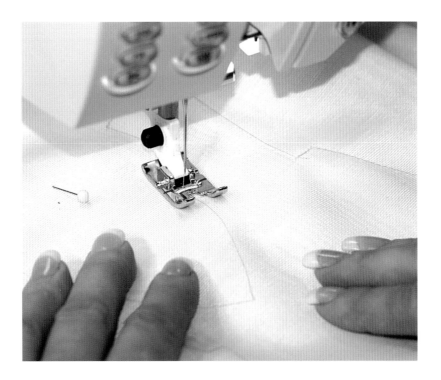

3. Trim around the pieces leaving a ¼" seam allowance.

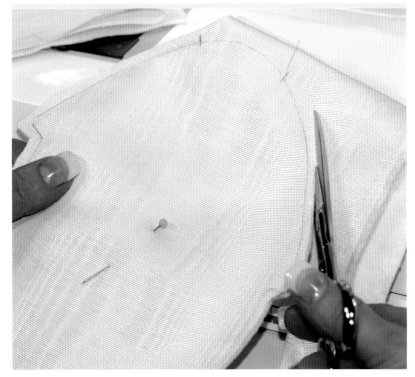

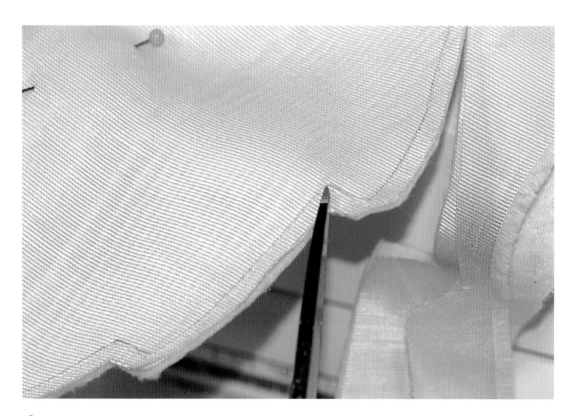

4. It's very important to clip the inside angles close to the stitching line, and snip the outside points to reduce bulk for turning, creating a shapelier leaf or petal.

5. Turn all the leaves and petals right side out and press flat.

6. Using the embroidery thread, stitch the "veins" on the leaves and flower petals (we used 40wt Sulky® 2113, vari-bright green, on petals and Sulky®1177, avocado, for the leaves). Starting and ending the stitching at the bottom edge of the petals will allow you to sew the veins using a continuous stitch-out. For example, starting at the bottom edge, stitch the center vein to the top of the leaf. You can lightly trace the vein lines on the fabric, or feel free to be creative and freehand stitch! Pivot the leaf at the top and stitch back down the same stitching to the point where you would pivot to turn to create the first vein. Stitch the first vein, pivoting near the outside edge and stitching back over the previous stitching to the center vein. Continue this process back and forth across the petal to the bottom of the leaf, stitching each vein as you come upon it.

7. Cut two 17" squares for the pillow top and back, using the pattern, if desired. Follow the Bottom Edge Insertion instructions found on page 32 to insert the zipper.

8. Print out the pillow top template from the CD-ROM. This will be used to help you with petal and leaf placement on the pillow top. Use a sharp crafts knife or seam ripper to cut slits through the dotted leaf placement lines. Center the template on top of one 17" square and mark the stitching lines for each of the leaves and flower petals through the template using a air-soluble marking pen.

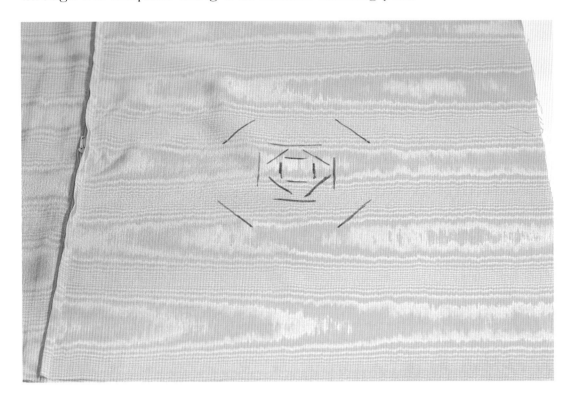

9. With right sides together (vein side down), match the raw edge of a leaf to the outside placement line as shown, and sew ¼" seam.

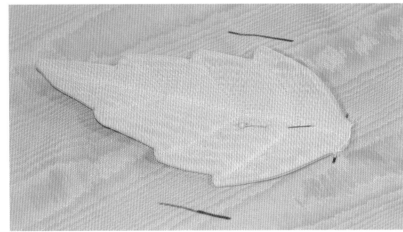

10. Fold the leaf back, and stitch next to the fold a scant ¼" from the edge.

11. Continue stitching all four leaves in the same manner.

12. The four large, four medium, and four small petals are sewn on using the same technique as the leaves. Start with the largest petals on top of the leaves and graduate the size down.

13. After all the petals are sewn in place, make the covered button for the center following the manufacturer's instructions. We added jewels to the button and pillow top, using the L'orna® Decorative Touch™ Wand and Gold Rhine Studs. If these are not available to you, try using glue with beads or glitter.

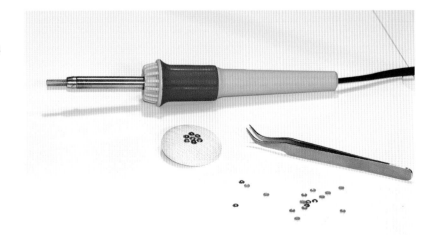

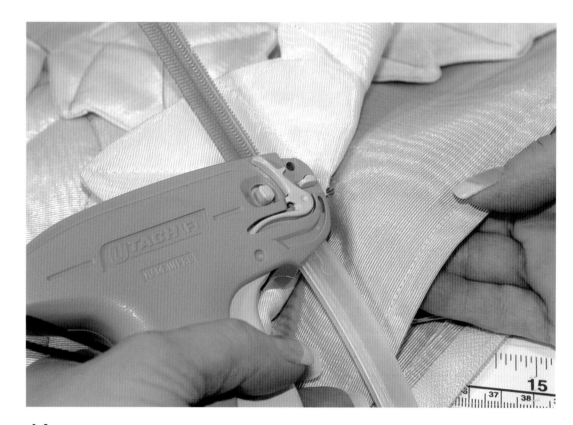

14. To keep the petals from flopping forward, but still looking loose and three-dimensional, use a quilter's basting gun, or sew some loose stitches through the leaves to keep the petals in place.

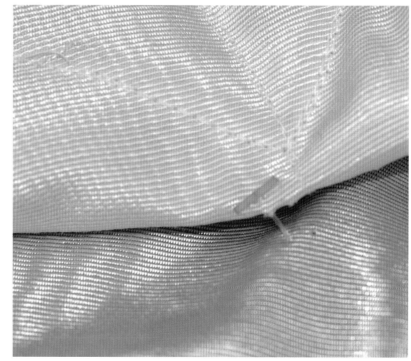

15. With right sides together, sew the three remaining sides of the pillow together using a ½" seam and sewing over the zipper tape. Serge the seam allowance to create a professional finish. Open the zipper, turn right side out, and stuff with the 16"-square pillow form.

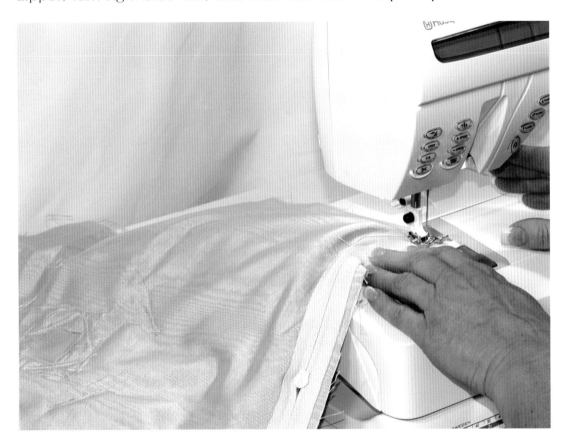

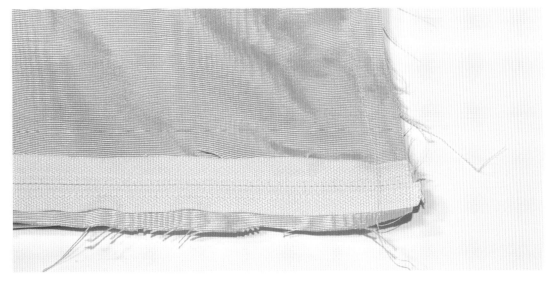

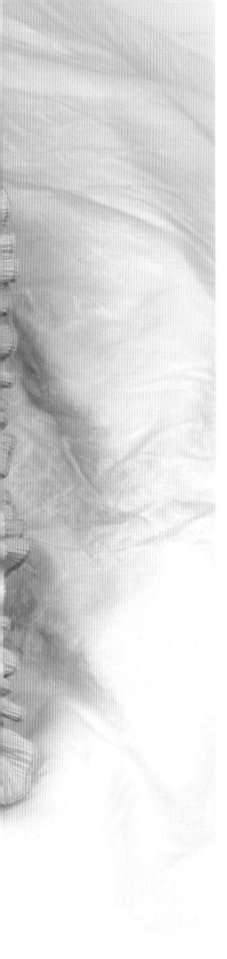

The Bloomin' Pillow

This project is designed with the ruffler in mind! If your foot doesn't resemble these shown, it may be a gathering foot and not a ruffler. For home decorating fabric projects, the ruffler is a must-have. You may make this project without the ruffler by using a zigzag stitch over a thin cord, but keep in mind it will take much longer to sew. This pillow was so much fun to make that you'll want to make a bunch of these! Use your ruffler in a new and creative way and make your own bloomin' bouquet!

Materials:

- 2 yards of home decorating fabric
- 18" zipper tape, with slide
- Ruffler attachment
- Zipper foot
- 5mm rolled hem foot
- Matching thread
- 16"-square pillow form

A SPECIAL TIME

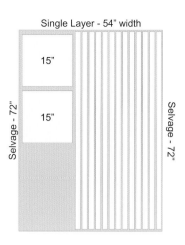

Single Layer - 54" width

Selvage - 72"

15"

15"

Selvage - 72"

Cut:

Print the stitching template on your computer's printer from the CD-ROM. For the pillow body, cut two 15" squares. Cut 26 yards of 3" strips (13 strips, each 72" long) for the ruffles.

1. Sew the ruffle strips together and serge one edge with a rolled hem or zigzag to finish. Using the ruffler attachment on your sewing machine, ruffle at a fullness of approximately 3 1/4 to 3 1/2 times. For example: 20" of flat ruffle will be 5 3/4" to 6" after being ruffled. The stitch to pleat ratio must be set at 1 and the set screw screwed almost all the way down. It's advisable to ruffle a few samples of leftover project fabric before beginning on your ruffle, to adjust the settings.

2. With the right side up, trim the beginning ruffle end to make a gentle curve as shown.

Hint: To tighten or gather the ruffle more, turn the set screw to the right. To loosen the gathers, turn the set screw to the left. Remember: "Righty, tighty; lefty, loosey!"

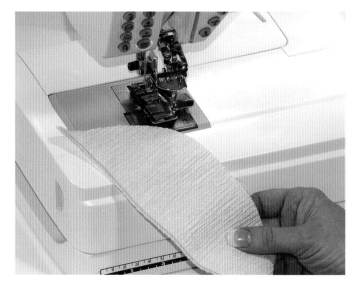

3. Place the fabric edge in the ruffler between the two layers of black feed teeth. Use the fabric guide under the ruffler as shown. You will need approximately 6½ to 7 yards of finished ruffle to complete the top of the pillow.

4. Transfer the stitching lines to the right side of the pillow front from the template printed from the CD. Using a sharp blade, cut slits in the pattern and trace. These stitching lines are only a guide, so if your stitching varies a little, don't push the panic button. You'll be fine!

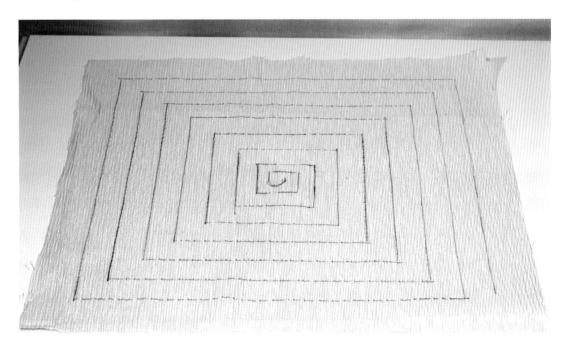

5. Begin by rolling the first few inches of the ruffle and sewing it at the center of the stitching diagram.

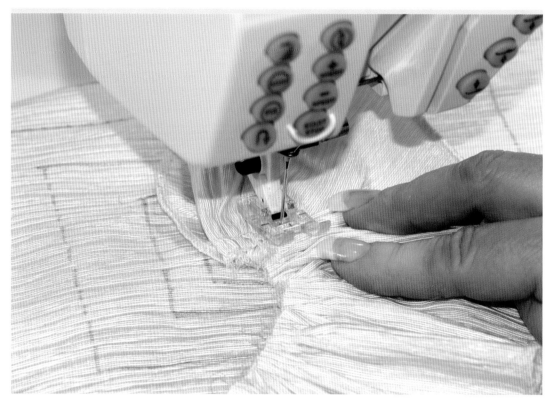

6. Keep the ruffle very full in the center of the pillow. In order to do this, push extra ruffle under the presser foot as you sew.

7. Follow the drawn lines, stitching down the ruffle until you get to the end.

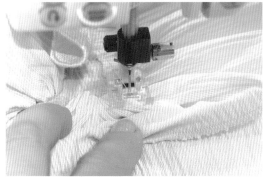

8. Finish by tucking under the serged edge as shown.

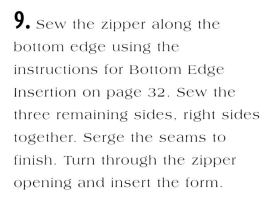

9. Sew the zipper along the bottom edge using the instructions for Bottom Edge Insertion on page 32. Sew the three remaining sides, right sides together. Serge the seams to finish. Turn through the zipper opening and insert the form.

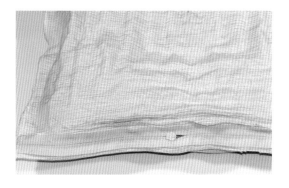

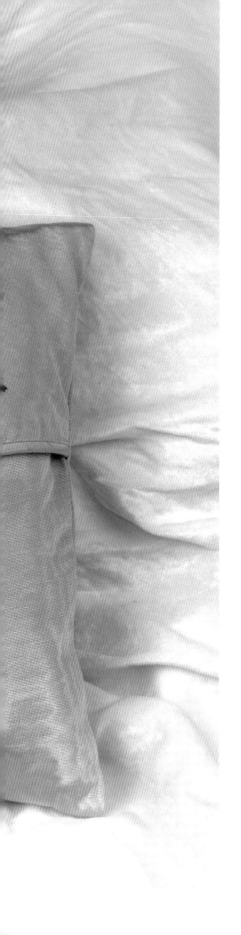

Snow
Let It

e dedicate this pillow to everyone who loves snowflakes. If you've ever made an envelope pillow and had the flap stick out like it was saluting you, then you'll love this tip. Katie and I learned this the hard way, too! We found that by cutting the flap smaller at the bottom edge, the flap hugs the pillow and lies flat.

Materials:

- 1 yard of fabric
- 5/8 yard of 1/4" welt cord
- 12"x16" pillow form
- Matching thread
- Single welt foot

Embroidery Supplies:

- Hoop Size: 360mm x 150mm Mega Hoop
- Stabilizer: Sulky® Cut-Away Plus™
- Coordinating metallic embroidery thread

Cut:

Cut a rectangle 36"x18". Print on your computer's printer the flap pattern from the CD-ROM. This will be the facing for your envelope flap.

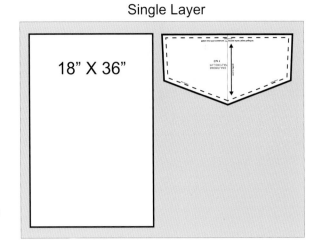

Single Layer

18" X 36"

1. From the leftover fabric, make approximately 20" of ¼" welt cord using the instructions for Making Welting found on page 20.

2. Embroider the snowflake design on one end of the 36"x18" rectangle, using the Sulky® Cut-Away Plus™ stabilizer and metallic thread. Center your design between 4" to 4½" from the edge on the 18"

end of fabric. You want the edge of the embroidery design to stitch out no more than 2" from the edge of the pillow fabric. After embroidering, trim the stabilizer from the back of the pillow, and press. If you choose not to embroider a design, proceed to the next step. With right sides together and raw edges even, sew the ¼" welt cord onto the angled side of the facing, clipping the corded seam at the point while sewing.

3. Next, clean-finish or serge along the top straight edge of the flap. Find the center of the embroidered end and mark with a pin. An extra 1" has been added to the width, and 3½" added to the length to adjust the size after the embroidery is completed. With right sides together, center the point of the flap facing on the center of the embroidery. Pin in place and sew the welt edge only. A welt foot comes in handy here! If you don't have a welt foot, use a zipper foot so you can stitch close to the welt cord.

4. Trim the pillow sides except for the flap to measure 17" across. The flap piece already has a gentle taper to make it ½" narrower at the lower edges. We need to keep the taper in the facing, as it keeps the flap from tenting out and helps hug the pillow. Note: Trim from both sides equally to keep the embroidery and flap centered. You will trim approximately ½" from each side, depending on where your center point is. Trim the length to 32" from the flap point, as shown. Serge the straight end.

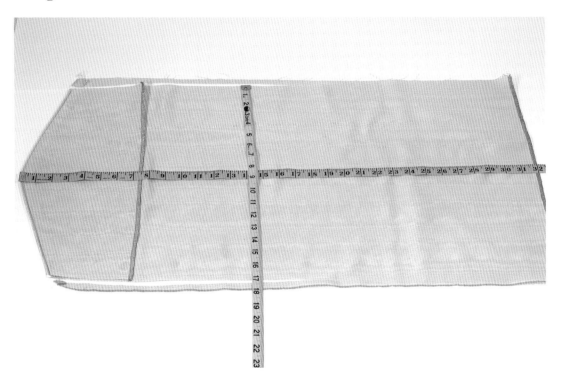

5. Sew the flap down first, aligning the tapered edges so they are even with the raw edges of the pillow body, as shown.

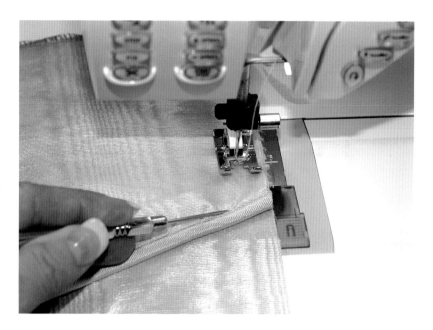

6. Fold the pillow body up 12", with the facing to the inside, making an envelope. Sew the side seams in place. Serge the side seam allowances and turn to the right side. Stuff the envelope with the pillow form.

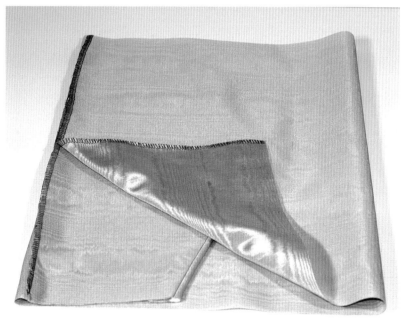

Ring Bearer's Pillows

A wedding is a deeply personal and emotional time, with every detail of the utmost importance. We decided to make a collection of ring bearer's pillows that could appeal to every bride. Whether your ceremony is civil or religious, large or small, you're sure to want one of these pillows to carry your token of love.

Make this pillow your own by choosing the color of the fabric to match your gown— white, ivory, or pastel; choose the shape— an oval, diamond, or rectangle from the patterns on the CD-ROM; choose your center embroidery—monogram, cross, or Star of David; and choose the metallic threads to match your rings—silver or gold. Each pillow has either a small twisted cord or ribbon on each side to tie the wedding rings to the pillow.

Once you have chosen the pillow shape, you must decide whether to use the optional embroideries or not. If you do not own an embroidery machine, embellishments can be done by hand, or you may choose to add lace appliqués to match your wedding dress, or purchase some of the many ready-made types of embroidery available. You may also decide to sew pearls or crystal beads to the pillow top. Personalizing your pillow will make it that much more special!

Oval Pillow

Materials:

Supplies appropriate for any shape

- ³/₈ yard of moiré or similar home decorating fabric
- Gold or silver metallic thread
- Matching embroidery thread
- Polyester batting to fill pillow
- Single welt foot
- Optional: four tassels

Embroidery Supplies:

- Hoop Size: 240mm x 150mm hoop
- Stabilizer: Sulky® Totally Stable™ Iron-on Tear-Away Stabilizer
- Coordinating 40wt rayon embroidery thread

The oval pillow is the most difficult of the three shapes to make. After cutting out the pattern and adding any desired embellishments, add a welt cord to the front edge. Although a welt cord edge is not necessary for the rectangular or diamond-shape pillows, it will help shape the edge of the oval pillow.

Cut:

Print the oval pattern found on the CD-ROM using your computer's printer. Cut two layers at one time. From the remaining fabric, cut enough 2" bias for the outside edge of the pillow plus 6" for the hand strap on the back side of the pillow. Review the information on Making Continuous Bias found on page 18.

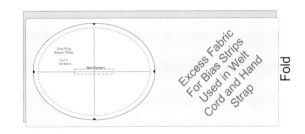

1. Embellish the pillow front as desired. Note: If you are planning to use any of the embroidery designs on the CD-ROM, trace the oval pattern on a larger rectangular piece of fabric first, stitch the design, and then use the oval pattern to cut out the pillow. This will help keep the fabric from distorting and allow you to center the embroidery design before stitching the pillow together. To do this, match up the embroidery alignment marks from the pattern that you drew on the fabric with the pattern embroidery alignment marks, prior to cutting.

2. Sew the welt cord along the edge following the instructions found on page 20 for Making Welting. Tack down the corded ring ties near each of the embroideries (see instructions for Making Ring Ties on page 141). Use the handle placement guide on the pattern for placement. Secure each tie with a bar tack or small zigzag stitch in the center of the cording/ribbon.

3. Cut 2" bias strips from the leftover fabric to make a bias tube. Begin with right sides together then sew along the long edge for about 6". Trim to 5", turn, and press flat. Turn under ½" at each end of the strap and center on the pillow back using the placement guide on the oval pattern. Stitch the ends close to the folds to secure. This will give you a strap for the ring bearer to put his/her hand through.

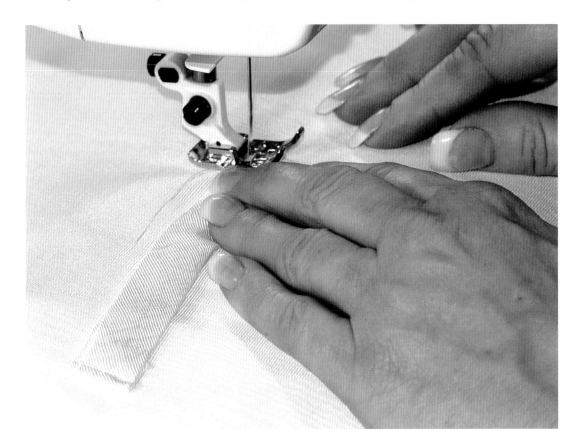

4. Sew the pillow front to the back, right sides together, matching the notches and leaving an opening of about 5" for turning. Before turning right side out, stitch a ribbon or twill tape in the seam to slightly gather the outside edge. You will want to hold the ribbon or twill tape taut while sewing. This will give the welt cord edge a smooth finish when the pillow is stuffed. Review the instructions for this technique found in the PETAL PUSHER pillow on page 42. Turn right side out, stuff the pillow, and slipstitch the opening closed.

A SPECIAL TIME

Diamond
Pillow

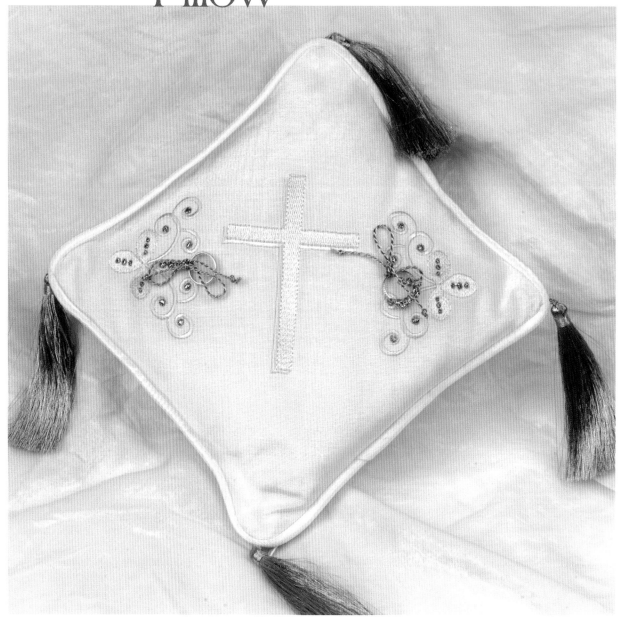

This pillow uses the same embroidery instructions as the oval pillow, but after the embroidery is finished, cut a diamond shape.

Cut:

Cut a 13½"x13½" square for the front of the pillow. Using the pattern found on the CD-ROM, mark the embroidery alignment lines on the fabric square and embroider the design of your choice on the fabric. After

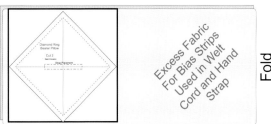

completing the embroidery, match up the embroidery alignment marks from the fabric with the pattern embroidery alignment marks, then cut your diamond-shape pillow. This will also help center the embroidery design on the pillow accurately.

1. Once the pillow top has been embellished, cut to 9"x9". Cut a 9" square for the pillow back. If there is a lot of embellishment added, the size and shape of the pillow can become distorted. Trimming up and matching to the pillow back, before sewing together or adding welt cord, will ensure a nicely conformed diamond-shape pillow. Add ribbons or cord to tie the rings, following the instructions for Making Ring Ties on page 141.

2. If you're adding welt cord to your pillow, make and sew the welt cord using the instructions found on page 20 for Making Welting. Sew the welt cord to the pillow top. Trim the top to match the pillow back.

3. Follow the instructions in Step 3 of the Oval Ring Bearer's Pillow for making the strap for the back.

4. Sew the pillow front to the back, right sides together, matching the corners and leaving an opening of about 5" along one side for turning right side out. Turn, stuff the pillow, and slipstitch closed.

Rectangular
Pillow

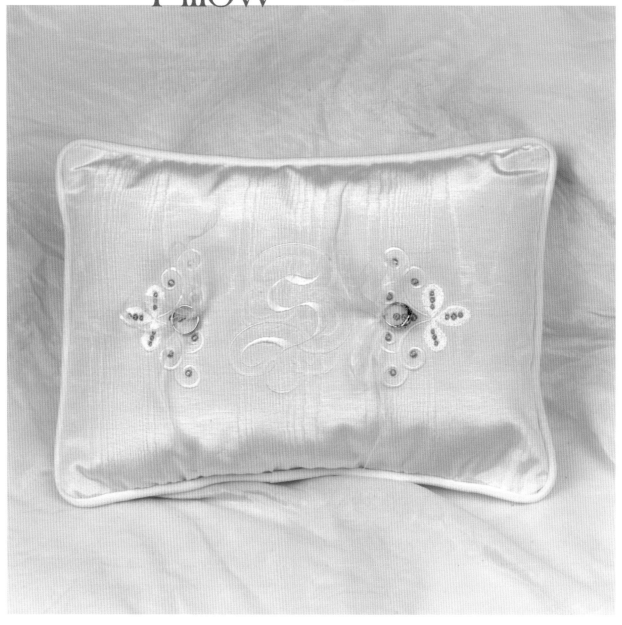

or the rectangle-shape and diamond-shape pillows, you may choose to insert a zipper in the bottom edge, using the insertion method of your choice found on pages 28 – 33.

Cut:

Cut two 10"x13" rectangles using the pattern pieces from the CD-ROM. Cut 2" bias from the remaining fabric to trim the pillow, plus an additional 6" of bias for the hand strap.

1. Embellish the pillow top as desired. If you use one of the elegant embroidery designs on the CD-ROM, use the embroidery alignment lines on the pattern to help you center your design on the pillow. Refer to the steps for the oval- and diamond-shape Ring Bearer's Pillows to trim and center the embroidery on the pillow.

2. Add ribbons or cord to tie down the rings. Follow the Making Ring Ties instructions below. Trim the pillow top edges with welt cord or a purchased trim of your choice.

3. The pillow back is finished just like the Diamond Pillow, steps 3 and 4. Turn right side out, stuff the pillow, and slipstitch closed.

Making Ring Ties:

With this method you twist two, four, or several cords or threads together to make a thicker cord. To make the ties, start with an ample supply of thread or cord. We used eight strands, four times the desired finished length.

Tie the thread tails in a knot and thread through the hole in the center of a bobbin. Put the bobbin on the bobbin winder of your sewing machine. While holding the ends very tight, engage the bobbin winder until the thread twists very tight and until the thread shortens about 10% to 15%. Find the center of these twisted threads, pull toward you to fold in half, and release the end. The threads will twist upon themselves, creating your custom cording. Knot the ends to keep the threads from fraying. Set aside to use for ring ties.

party !
my room
2 A.M.
B.Y.O.B.

It's Party Time

This project is a great gift for that "mother-to-be" and will surely get a laugh or two at a baby shower or christening party. The home-made fringe is constructed in the embroidery hoop, but you can improvise with a long satin stitch if you don't have access to an embroidery machine. The twisted cord hanger is made from 12wt cotton embroidery thread using the Making Ring Ties technique found on page 141. Caution is advised, as this project can spawn many other creative ideas. Before you know it, everyone in the household will want their own personal door pillows!

Materials:
- ¼ yard of fabric
- Coordinating 12wt rayon embroidery thread for hanger
- Polyester fiberfill

Embroidery Supplies:
- Hoop Size: 100mm x 100mm hoop
- Stabilizer: Sulky® Totally Stable™ Iron-on Tear-Away Stablilizer or Sulky® Paper Solvy
- Water-soluble basting thread for bobbin
- Coordinating 40wt rayon embroidery thread

Cut:

Cut two 8" squares from the fabric.

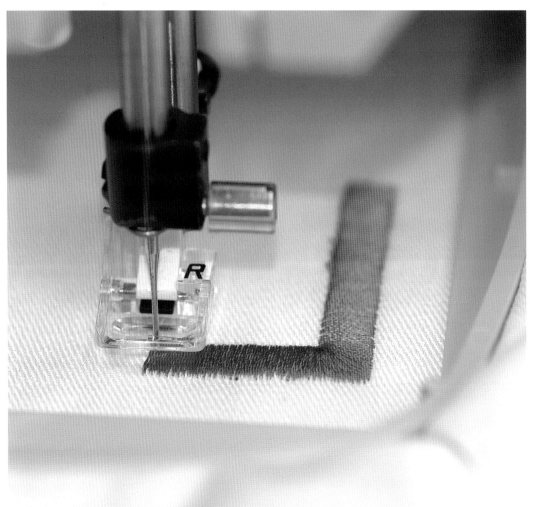

1. To make the fringe, hoop your stabilizer and fabric centering the design on one 8" square. By using the Paper Solvy, the stabilizer will dissolve in water after creating the fringe. For the first embroidery color, make sure you have the water-soluble basting thread in the bobbin. Embroider the design through the first color only.

2. The second color stop is placed in the design so you remember to put your regular embroidery bobbin thread back into the machine. Once you replace the bobbin thread, continue embroidering the small satin border that secures the fringe in place. (Note: If you forget to replace the water-soluble bobbin thread with regular bobbin thread at this point, you won't forget in the future. Especially when you soak your project and all the threads come out! Ask Katie how she knows!)

3. You can continue to stitch through the third and final color the lettering with the same thread color, as we did in our sample, or you can be creative and change the thread color.

4. To release the fringe, remove the fabric and stabilizer from the hoop. Remove any excess stabilizer and soak the piece in warm water to remove the Paper Solvy stabilizer, as well as the water-soluble basting thread that is temporarily holding the fringe in place. Rinse the piece completely and dry thoroughly. When your fabric is dry, pull the threads to the top of the design to create the fringe. (Note: A stiletto is a useful tool to help you get all the threads to the top.) The small satin internal border will keep the fringe in place and keep it from coming undone. It's like magic!

5. When all the fringe is released, draw a line around the square, 1" away from the inner border stitching line, creating a 5½" square. Cut the pillow back fabric to match the pillow top along the drawn lines.

6. Before sewing the front to the back, create your own cording for the hanger. This method uses the over-twisting of one, two, or several cords or threads to make a thicker cord. To begin, you will need ample lengths of thread; we used eight strands, approximately four times the desired finished length. Tie the thread tails in a knot and thread through the hole in the center of a bobbin. Put the bobbin on the bobbin winder of your sewing machine. While holding the ends very tight, begin winding slowly until the thread twists very tight and the thread shortens about 10% to 15%. Find the center of the twisted threads, pull toward you to fold in half, and release the end. The cording will twist upon itself making a simple, elegant cord trim. Knot the ends to keep the trim from the fraying. Set aside.

7. With right sides of together and with the bulk of the cord hanger to the inside, place a hanger end in each of the top corners of the pillow. Begin sewing a ½" seam on the bottom edge leaving a 2" opening to stuff the pillow.

8. Trim the corners and turn the pillow right side out. Press flat and stuff with fiberfill as desired. Slipstitch the opening closed and hang the pillow on your door. It's Party Time!

About the CD-ROM

To access the information on the CD-ROM, place the CD-ROM in your CD drive and view the contents using Windows Explorer. If the contents of the CD do not automatically open into a window, click on your Start button and open MY COMPUTER. In MY COMPUTER, double-click on the appropriate CD-ROM drive to open a window to access the contents.

Each chapter in the book will coincide with a Directory/Folder on the CD-ROM. You can find the embroidery files and/or patterns corresponding to each project in the appropriate chapter folder. The compatible embroidery formats will each be in their individual folders for copying to your sewing machine via your normal methods.

You will find the Adobe Acrobat Reader install file in the Adobe file folder.

You will find the Notions Order Form in the Notions folder.

Embroidery Designs available on the CD-ROM:

Flower Power

My Hero

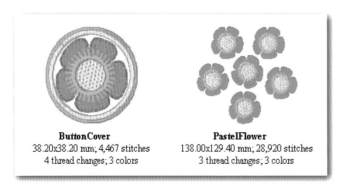

ButtonCover
38.20x38.20 mm; 4,467 stitches
4 thread changes; 3 colors

PastelFlower
138.00x129.40 mm; 28,920 stitches
3 thread changes; 3 colors

MyHero
148.00x47.60 mm; 2,449 stitches
1 thread changes; 1 colors

Quilted Celtic Elegance

QuiltedCelti
129.80x150.20 mm; 26,158 stitches
3 thread changes; 2 colors

QuiltedRecta
144.00x354.80 mm; 4,932 stitches
1 thread changes; 1 colors

Katie's Gone Loopy!

LoopyBorder
46.20x160.80 mm; 4,404 stitches
1 thread changes; 1 colors

Endless Leaves

EndlessLeaves
52.00x155.20 mm; 740 stitches
1 thread changes; 1 colors

Let It Snow

SnowFlakes
139.80x317.60 mm; 24,498 stitches
1 thread changes; 1 colors

It's Party Time

PartyMyRoom
98.20x97.00 mm; 9,821 stitches
3 thread changes; 3 colors

Monogrammed Neckroll / Tassels Abound

A_100
89.10x85.90 mm; 5,585 stitches
1 thread changes; 1 colors

B_100
79.40x94.20 mm; 5,760 stitches
1 thread changes; 1 colors

C_100
76.60x88.40 mm; 5,501 stitches
1 thread changes; 1 colors

D_100
72.40x92.00 mm; 5,644 stitches
1 thread changes; 1 colors

E_100
76.40x94.80 mm; 6,168 stitches
1 thread changes; 1 colors

F_100
69.60x90.80 mm; 5,912 stitches
1 thread changes; 1 colors

G_100
90.90x93.60 mm; 6,211 stitches
1 thread changes; 1 colors

H_100
73.40x95.40 mm; 5,442 stitches
1 thread changes; 1 colors

I_100
62.80x91.00 mm; 5,203 stitches
1 thread changes; 1 colors

J_100
62.00x89.80 mm; 4,979 stitches
1 thread changes; 1 colors

K_100
81.00x90.80 mm; 5,761 stitches
1 thread changes; 1 colors

L_100
79.00x92.20 mm; 5,964 stitches
1 thread changes; 1 colors

M_100
91.40x86.40 mm; 7,196 stitches
1 thread changes; 1 colors

N_100
90.40x86.20 mm; 5,998 stitches
1 thread changes; 1 colors

O_100
90.60x86.20 mm; 6,081 stitches
1 thread changes; 1 colors

P_100
85.60x92.60 mm; 6,677 stitches
1 thread changes; 1 colors

Q_100
81.40x94.00 mm; 5,249 stitches
1 thread changes; 1 colors

R_100
77.00x95.20 mm; 6,019 stitches
1 thread changes; 1 colors

S_100
73.40x89.00 mm; 5,475 stitches
1 thread changes; 1 colors

T_100
76.80x93.00 mm; 5,760 stitches
1 thread changes; 1 colors

U_100
80.60x94.80 mm; 5,720 stitches
1 thread changes; 1 colors

V_100
67.60x93.20 mm; 5,345 stitches
1 thread changes; 1 colors

W_100
89.60x91.80 mm; 7,000 stitches
1 thread changes; 1 colors

X_100
74.20x94.40 mm; 5,334 stitches
1 thread changes; 1 colors

Y_100
72.40x94.60 mm; 5,982 stitches
1 thread changes; 1 colors

Z_100
70.40x92.80 mm; 5,190 stitches
1 thread changes; 1 colors

Ring Bearer's Pillows

Cross

Cross
121.00x220.00 mm; 19,962 stitches
3 thread changes; 3 colors

Star

Star
87.80x220.00 mm; 21,075 stitches
4 thread changes; 3 colors

Ring Bearer's Pillows

Mono_A
87.80x220.00 mm; 19,270 stitches
3 thread changes; 3 colors

Mono_B
94.20x220.00 mm; 19,445 stitches
3 thread changes; 3 colors

Mono_C
88.40x220.00 mm; 19,186 stitches
3 thread changes; 3 colors

Mono_D
92.00x220.00 mm; 19,329 stitches
3 thread changes; 3 colors

Mono_E
94.80x220.00 mm; 19,853 stitches
3 thread changes; 3 colors

Mono_F
90.80x220.00 mm; 19,597 stitches
3 thread changes; 3 colors

Mono_G
93.60x220.00 mm; 19,896 stitches
3 thread changes; 3 colors

Mono_H
95.40x220.00 mm; 19,127 stitches
3 thread changes; 3 colors

Mono_I
91.00x220.00 mm; 18,888 stitches
3 thread changes; 3 colors

Mono_J
89.80x220.00 mm; 18,664 stitches
3 thread changes; 3 colors

Mono_K
90.80x220.00 mm; 19,446 stitches
3 thread changes; 3 colors

Mono_L
92.20x220.00 mm; 19,649 stitches
3 thread changes; 3 colors

Mono_M
87.80x220.00 mm; 20,881 stitches
3 thread changes; 3 colors

Mono_N
87.80x220.00 mm; 19,683 stitches
3 thread changes; 3 colors

Mono_O
87.80x220.00 mm; 19,766 stitches
3 thread changes; 3 colors

Mono_P
92.60x220.00 mm; 20,362 stitches
3 thread changes; 3 colors

Mono_Q
94.00x220.00 mm; 18,934 stitches
3 thread changes; 3 colors

Mono_R
95.20x220.00 mm; 19,704 stitches
3 thread changes; 3 colors

Mono_S
89.00x220.00 mm; 19,160 stitches
3 thread changes; 3 colors

Mono_T
93.00x220.00 mm; 19,445 stitches
3 thread changes; 3 colors

Mono_U
94.80x220.00 mm; 19,405 stitches
3 thread changes; 3 colors

Mono_V
93.20x220.00 mm; 19,030 stitches
3 thread changes; 3 colors

Mono_W
91.80x220.00 mm; 20,685 stitches
3 thread changes; 3 colors

Mono_X
94.40x220.00 mm; 19,019 stitches
3 thread changes; 3 colors

Mono_Y
94.60x220.00 mm; 19,667 stitches
3 thread changes; 3 colors

Mono_Z
92.80x220.00 mm; 18,875 stitches
3 thread changes; 3 colors

Acknowledgements

We gratefully acknowledge the following companies for their support and contribution toward the production of this book. We hope you continue to support these companies by purchasing their products at your local sewing machine dealer and fabric store.

June Tailor -
White Colorfast Printer Fabric
P.O. Box 208
2861 Highway 175
Richfield, WI 53076
1-800-844-5400
www.junetailor.com

Havel's™ Incorporated –
Ultra-Pro Seam Ripper
3726 Lonsdale Street
Cincinnati, OH 45227
1-800-638-4770
www.havels.com

The Crowning Touch, Inc. -
The Fasturn® Tools for Turning Fabric Tubes!
3859 S Stage Road
Medford, OR 97501
1-800-729-0280
www.crowning-touch.com

Prym-Dritz Corporation –
Covered Button Kits – Size 60
P.O. Box 5028
Spartanburg, SC 29304
1-800-255-7796
www.dritz.com

Kandi Corp. –
L'orna® Decorative Touch™ Wand
PO Box 8345
Clearwater, FL 33758
1-800-985-2634
www.kandicorp.com

Gingher –
Embroidery scissors and fabric shears
322-D Edwardia Drive
Greensboro, NC 27409
1-800-446-4437
www.gingher.com

(H) Husqvarna VIKING

Viking Sewing Machines Inc.
31000 Viking Parkway
Westlake, OH 44145
1-800-358-0001
www.husqvarnaviking.com

PFAFF

Pfaff Sewing Machines
P.O. Box 458012
Westlake, OH 44145
1-440-808-6550
www.pfaffusa.com

BERNINA®

Bernina of America
3500 Thayer Court
Aurora, IL 60504-6182
1-800-405-2SEW
www.berninausa.com

Sulky® of America –
Thread and Stablizer
PO Box 494129
Port Charlotte, FL 33949-4129
1- 800-874-4115
www.sulky.com

To order any specialty products used in this book, please visit our Websites:
www.Kjbartz.com or
www.Pamdamour.com

INDEX